TRUST

TRUST

KNOWING WHEN TO GIVE IT,
WHEN TO WITHHOLD IT,
HOW TO EARN IT, AND HOW TO
FIX IT WHEN IT GETS BROKEN

HENRY CLOUD

WORTHY
PUBLISHING

NASHVILLE   NEW YORK

Worthy
Hachette Book Group
1290 Avenue of the Americas, New York, NY 10104
worthypublishing.com
twitter.com/worthypub

First Edition: March 2023

Worthy is a division of Hachette Book Group, Inc. The Worthy name and logo are
trademarks of Hachette Book Group, Inc.

The publisher is not responsible for websites (or their content) that are not
owned by the publisher.

Worthy Books may be purchased in bulk for business, educational, or promotional
use. For information, please contact your local bookseller or the Hachette Book
Group Special Markets Department at special.markets@hbgusa.com.

Library of Congress Control Number: 2022949174

Interior book design by Timothy Shaner, NightandDayDesign.biz

ISBNs: 9781546003373 (hardcover), 9781546003403 (ebook)

Printed in the United States of America

LSC-C

Printing 1, 2023

This book is dedicated to Tori,
the most trustworthy person I know.

CONTENTS

CONTENTS

TRUST

INTRODUCTION

"**J**ust trust me."

We've all heard these three words, and we've probably spoken them. Some people speak them fully expecting others to immediately say, "Of course, I'll trust you. This will be great!" Perhaps we have said them and meant well, but without understanding how much we were truly asking of another person or even not knowing exactly how to make good on the commitments that their trust would require of us. Perhaps we let them down unintentionally because we didn't understand how much we were asking them to risk with the brief statement: "Just trust me."

I think "Just trust me" should come with sirens, flashing lights, and other warning signs. These words often fall short. They can disappoint, sometimes terribly. Neuroscience tells us there's a good reason we should not "just trust" someone. I'll explain this in greater detail in this book, but suffice it here to say that the entire human nervous system and brain are wired to scan our environment and quickly assess each person with whom we interact. We are designed to ask one crucial question before any other: Is it safe? When someone invites us to trust, we want to know before anything else if we will get hurt. And we'll work hard to avoid pain.

The answer to the question "Is it safe" begins in milliseconds, but it can determine the future of a personal relationship, a family, a business deal, or an entire company. Why? Because trust sends a signal to our entire being that says, "Move forward." When we trust, we move toward a person, a group, a deal, a company, or whatever the object of our trust may be, and invest our hearts, time, energy, love, or wallets. When we don't trust, we get a strong internal message in the opposite direction: "Move away." Every day, in a thousand ways, with every personal and business encounter, we decide either to move toward or to move away.

In your personal life, everything rises and falls on trust. Trust yields intimacy. You could probably write your own book about the benefits of being in a relationship with a truly trustworthy person as well as the devastation of realizing you couldn't really trust someone. Likewise, in business, trust is everything. Businesspeople want others to trust them, to move toward them, because trust fuels investment.

Whether you're dealing with a marriage partner, a friend, your team at work, your customers, your partner, or your employees, you want them to invest their hearts, minds, energy, and resources with you. For them to make that investment and make it freely, you must deliver trust—not just once, but over and over. Yet, I think everyone has risked trusting someone in the past and wished they hadn't.

———

We can become better and better at knowing who is trustworthy and who is not. And we can get better at deciding when and with whom we will put ourselves at risk.

———

Probably everyone reading this book, including me, has been victimized by a betrayal, small or large, that still stings. We all have our stories of misplaced trust. We either missed warning signs and moved forward when we shouldn't have, or worse, the warning signs were not visible. Everything about a situation looked good on the surface, and maybe it was, but we got burned anyway. When we look back, we say to ourselves, "I just didn't see that coming." Or, "How could they have done that to me? We were such good friends [or lovers, or partners]. How could they have treated me that way?" And sometimes it is not even an actual "betrayal" but someone's "honest inability" to do what we needed. We don't have good answers, but we do have scars.

I cannot promise you that you will never be betrayed or let down again after reading this book. Even God cannot make that guarantee. Every day He extends trust to humans who let him down or even reject Him. At one point, He even said He was sorry He created us:

> So the LORD was sorry he had ever made them and put them
> on the earth. It broke his heart. —Genesis 6:6 NLT

Most of us can echo this sentiment. Surely you have had the thought: "I am *so* sorry I trusted that person. It broke my heart." Or other aspects of our lives.

But here is the good news: *We can become better and better at knowing who is trustworthy and who is not. And we can get better at deciding when and with whom we will put ourselves at risk.*

One of the goals of this book is to equip you to know how to "read between the lines" of what someone tells you, tries to sell you, or promises you and to be able to see what is trustworthy and what is not. In addition to assisting and guiding you as you develop this critical sense of judgment about whom to trust, I've designed this book to also help you:

- Understand the value of trust in every aspect of life and prioritize it in your efforts to be successful in love and life

- Determine who is trustworthy and who is not
- Identify and develop the attitudes, practices, and behaviors you need to become a trustworthy person for other people
- Run a business or organization that invites the trust of your customers or stakeholders
- Handle situations where someone has betrayed your trust
- Repair trust when it has been violated and broken, even when it feels broken beyond fixing
- Protect yourself in the process of rebuilding trust that has been broken
- Learn when not to trust again
- Discern the difference between trust and forgiveness

If I had to summarize in just a few words what this book is about, I would say this: *Trust is the fuel for all of life.* Nothing in life works without it—especially relationships. We are wired biologically, neurologically, emotionally, spiritually, and psychologically to trust. Trust is the currency that drives everything. So we need to be good at it.

The beloved Russian playwright Anton Chekhov said, "You must trust and believe in people or life becomes impossible." He's right. Typically, the words "Just trust me" mean nothing. For some people, they're even a red flag. In contrast, being trustworthy and being able to trust others means everything. Knowing whom to trust and how to trust will drastically impact every area of your life in astonishing and positive ways.

Do you want to build solid, healthy relationships because you can assess people effectively before you trust them, identify why and how trust is broken, and learn to repair valuable relationships that fall prey to misunderstanding or miscommunication? Do you want every aspect of your life and relationships to work? Then let's get started learning what makes trust work, how we can spot trustworthiness more clearly, and how we can grow in confidence as we move toward more deeply investing in the right people, companies, leaders, and institutions, both personally and professionally. After understanding how trust works, we'll look at how to repair it when something goes awry in a relationship. And what we will learn is that while observing the key traits of trustworthiness in others is a crucial aspect of getting good at when to trust (and when not to), we will also learn that who we are, what drives us, and what might be injured or incomplete in us are equally important. The process of trust, we will find, is also a journey of self-discovery. Join me as we begin growing in trust—the fuel for all of life.

SECTION 1

TRUST MAKES LIFE WORK

ONE

EVERYTHING DEPENDS ON TRUST

The morning was tense. I was accustomed to tense situations in my line of work, but I was not prepared for what happened next.

I had been called in to facilitate a crisis meeting. The board of directors of a global entity had convened in a last-ditch effort to save the company. A yearlong battle between the CEO and the board chair had reached a breaking point, and they had called an emergency board retreat to try to prevent what seemed inevitable—that one of the two executives would leave the company. The departure of either one would make global headlines. Hundreds of thousands of lives would be affected, and a great deal of money would be put at risk.

We began our day together by putting the issues on the table, ensuring that we were all starting with the same set of facts. The hope was to resolve the conflict between the two leaders so the company could continue to thrive. As best I could tell, based on my pre-meeting interviews, half of the board sided with the chair, and the other half with the CEO. And it was crystal clear that the two of them did not side with each other.

As each person shared their perspective, the tension was palpable, yet somewhat cordial. But soon, in a moment, it all turned dark. The CEO interrupted the chair to make a comment, and not in a polite or measured way. Then, it happened.

The board chair, with all eyes upon him, gently closed his portfolio. After looking down for a few seconds, he looked around the table and said to the group, "I am done. You all can take it from here, but I am done. Good luck."

With that, he got up and began walking toward the door. The room went silent with shock. I don't think anyone knew what to do, but they all knew that this was bad. The chairman was obviously resigning. He was walking out in the middle of the retreat intended to save the company.

I didn't know what to do, but I could not simply allow this devastating situation to continue. So I quickly ran across the room and placed myself between the chairman and the door. Then, I sat down on the floor and blocked his exit.

"Okay, wait," I said. "You can leave, but if you walk out this door, you will set into motion a chain of events that cannot be undone. It will affect hundreds of thousands of lives. Before you do that, I ask you this one thing. Please, sit down for a moment. Right here, with me."

There are times when people might think you are so crazy that they simply do what you ask them to do, and I think this was one of them. The chairman sat down on the floor, and I asked him, "What does it feel like when he does what he just did to you?"

He stared at me for a long moment and then began to speak. "I . . . I . . . just don't know . . . what . . ." And then his lower jaw began to quiver as he tried to speak. This powerful man, an acclaimed attorney and industry leader, could not get the words out. "He . . . he makes me feel like . . . There is no way . . . I can . . ."

Pain and emotion so saturated this man's words that he could no longer speak.

Within moments, movement across the room caught my attention. The CEO was walking over to us. He sat down beside us, looked at the chairman, and said, "I never knew I made you feel that way. I never knew. I would never want to make you feel that way. I am so, so sorry."

The chairman looked up and stared at the CEO for a moment. Then he turned to me, appearing as though he did not know what to say or do next.

I looked at the group and said, "Give me the room. I'll call you back in when we're ready."

Over the next hour and a half, the three of us simply talked. And listened, and talked some more. Finally, I invited the board to return and said, "Time to go to work."

For the remainder of the retreat, the board listened to the two executives talk about their disconnection and, more importantly, about how they would move forward. To say the least, things ended much better than they had been just a couple of hours earlier. Disaster averted.

The problem we have is this: we often don't understand how trust like theirs went awry, nor do we know the mechanisms involved to get back to a good place in the way they did. The goal of this book is to understand both: how it gets broken, and how to repair it when it does.

Can You Relate?

Perhaps you identify with the dynamics, the communication breakdowns, and the emotions expressed in this story. Maybe you are not a CEO or a board chair, but you fully understand tension, division, and skepticism in a relationship. You understand what it is like if it all breaks down or being caught in the middle between others where these problems exist. You know the heartache that comes from finding out someone you trusted has betrayed you or let you down. Your story may involve:

- The spouse you felt sure was loyal and totally devoted to you had an affair.
- The business partner with whom you entrusted your entire career sold out to your worst enemy.

- Someone you entrusted yourself to was not competent to do what you thought he or she would.
- The pastor with whom you entrusted your spiritual well-being was leading a double life.
- The friend with whom you shared your most intimate details spread your secrets to others.
- A beloved sibling turned against you in a battle over inheritance, and you were shocked to find that money or possessions could mean more to him or her than your relationship.
- The trusted employee in whom you invested much either started a new business without telling you or took valuable knowledge and expertise learned from you to work for a competitor.
- Your trusted teammate let you down.
- Someone you love was not capable of actually loving you in return in the ways you need it.

You know your history of broken trust. You know who was involved, and you know what happened. The list of ways humans can betray one another is almost infinite, but the pain is always the same: hurt, betrayal, disillusionment, anger, withdrawal from trusting others, reticence in future transactions, suspicion, and more. In short, when trust is broken and we are betrayed, we suffer.

Trust: More Than a Feeling

Trust is a familiar word and a familiar concept. We know what it means and when it's working for us. We also know, sometimes in agony, when it gets broken. Merriam-webster.com defines trust as a noun this way: "assured reliance on the character, ability, strength, or truth of someone or something." This is a good and accurate explanation of trust, but I really like how the Cambridge Dictionary defines *trust* as a verb: "to believe that someone is good and honest and will not harm you, or that something is safe and reliable." As I noted earlier, the crucial question we ask before we get involved with a person or a situation is, "Is it safe?" We long to feel safe and secure, and trust is the currency that brings those feelings about in our lives. When you put these two definitions together, it says a lot about what we are going to be looking at in this book. It is feeling safe—plus security that we can rely on someone to deliver what we need in several ways.

When you meet someone—a potential love interest, a potential employer or employee, a new neighbor, or a casual acquaintance—you often get a sense about that person, a feeling. You may say to yourself, "I seem to connect with her," or, "I don't know what it is, but I just don't feel good about that guy." You then tend to act upon those senses. The consequences of those actions may be as small as asking the person next to you at a ballgame to watch your jacket while you go to the restroom and seeing the jacket untouched when you return. Or they may be as life-altering as walking down the aisle with someone in marriage. In either case and in hundreds of others, you take the first step on the path of trust based on a feeling, and thereby you make yourself vulnerable to being hurt in some way. You place yourself at risk if the person you trust does not perform. Worse, if that person betrays your trust, you get hurt.

We are easily tempted to think that trust is simple, that we ought to be able to quickly spot a lack of trustworthiness. After all, we have seen cases where this was true. We have a family member who took a salesperson's word that the used car was reliable. We could immediately see that a friend's new boyfriend was narcissistic while she found him charming and liked his confidence. In both cases, we were amazed that the people we care about did not simply see what we saw. We frequently walk away from such instances feeling a bit smug, thinking, *How could he or she do that?* And for a moment, we feel a bit sturdier, saying to ourselves, "I wouldn't have let anyone take me for a ride like that. I'm smarter than that. I would have seen it." We feel like we are on the right side of Proverbs 22:3: "A prudent person foresees danger and takes precautions. The simpleton goes blindly on and suffers the consequences" (NLT).

While trust often begins with a feeling, it can't only be based on a feeling, an emotion, or some kind of sense. It has to be rooted in more solid, observable, essential qualities.

It's important for us to know that while trust often begins with a feeling, it can't only be based on a feeling, an emotion, or some kind of sense. It has to be rooted in more solid, observable, essential qualities, which we'll explore in part 2 of this book.

Believe It or Not, Trust Is Sexy

I had a client who said something powerful one day: "I never knew how sexy trust was." I found that statement intriguing, so I asked him to explain.

He had been put in a situation at work that would require him to be around a woman he had dated seriously before marrying his wife. He was concerned about how his wife would take this news and worried she would want him to refuse the project. Had he turned down the opportunity, it would have been really problematic for his work. He felt caught between two bad options.

But when he shared it with his wife, her response was surprising. "I am not worried about this at all. I totally trust you. Don't even think about it," she said.

This was good enough for him, because in reality, he had no designs on his former girlfriend to begin with. But he certainly understood how his being around her could be a problem for his wife.

He was surprised when he went on the first business trip that included his ex-girlfriend and found himself at a dinner meeting with her. Eventually, other attendees left the table, went to their rooms, and left him alone with the woman with whom he was once seriously involved. They talked for a while, and then the thought hit him: it would be so easy for him to cheat on his wife with her. Then he remembered how his wife trusted him, even though she knew he would have an opportunity to betray her, and she really, really trusted him.

As he sat there, he became even more aware of the depth of his wife's trust. He told me that, as he thought about it more and more, he felt he might explode inside with love and desire for her. He could hardly wait to end the dinner and get back to his room to call her. His heart and soul melted at the feeling of oneness that he had with his wife because of her trust in him.

Trust is the fuel for all of life.

That's why he said to me, "I never knew how sexy trust is. If I could have gotten to her at that moment. . . ." (I'll spare you the details, but you can imagine.) His wife's trust propelled him toward her and drove him more deeply into their relationship. Trust builds bonds, deepens them, and can call forth our greatest faithfulness. I'll explain the biochemical and psychological reasons for this in chapter 2.

What stood out for me about his story is exactly what I mentioned in the introduction to this book: *Trust is the fuel for all of life.* As I noted, we have been created and designed biologically, neurologically, emotionally, spiritually, and psychologically to trust. When we trust, life works. When trust is high, it gets all the juices flowing and everything runs well. When trust is low—well, you know what that's like. When trust is broken, things are even worse.

You've had enough experience with trust to realize that it's powerful. As I've stated, trust fuels all of life. That's why I'm on a campaign to persuade you to embrace trust and to grow in trust as one of the most important skills you can have.

Why Trust?

Let me offer several reasons trust matters so much and mention a few areas of life that depend on being able to trust:

- Physical and psychological maturity of the human organism, beginning at birth: brain size, body weight, immune system function, intellectual development, language and social development, and others.
- Trust in family of origin affects the ability to trust on all levels in adulthood, in marriage, and in other relationships.[*]
- Rises in trust affect gross domestic product (GDP) growth in economies through increases of business investment, human capital accumulation, and organizational improvements.
- Happily married couples trust that their spouse will "be there for them" when needed most. Unhappy couples do not have that same trust.[**]
- Couples therapy focusing on building emotional trust is more successful.[***]

---

[*] K. M. Franklin, R. Janoff-Bulman, and J. E. Roberts, "Long-Term Impact of Parental Divorce on Optimism and Trust: Changes in General Assumptions or Narrow Beliefs?" *Journal of Personality and Social Psychology* 59, no. 4 (1990): 743–55, https://doi.org/10.1037/0022-3514.59.4.743.\

[**] John M. Gottman, *The Science of Trust: Emotional Attunement for Couples* (New York: W. W. Norton & Company, 2011), 55. Kindle edition.

[***] Susan M. Johnson, *The Practice of Emotionally Focused Couple Therapy* (New York: Routledge, 2019).

- Work teams with high trust outperform teams with low trust in results across multiple measures.
- People higher in trust have better physical health and fewer health problems than those low in trust. Their high trust levels affect longevity and their mental health (lower anxiety and depression), and they are happier as people.
- High trust leaders are more effective across multiple measures.
- Physiological brain performance in marital relationships is reduced with low trust, resulting in lower conflict resolution and affecting divorce rates.
- Performance, turnover, and customer experience are affected by trust, and the absence of trust leads to multiple business problems.
- Trust built on empathy reduces anxiety across virtually all dimensions of life.
- Trust in surgical teams leads to better results and greater learning curves.
- Business marketing effectiveness is built upon the ability to create trust, and brand loyalty depends on it.
- What is referred to as "social trust" (positive attitudes toward other members of society) increases individual success; maintains health; reduces anxiety; increases welfare, health, and education; and improves physical and mental health in a society, while low trust does the opposite.[*]

The list could go on, but hopefully you see that trust matters greatly in every area of life, and you are becoming convinced that we all need it to do well.

---

[*] Farzin Rezaei et al. "The Relationship Between Spiritual Health and Social Trust Among Students," *Journal of Mind and Medical Sciences* 8, no. 1 (2021).

Researcher Roderick M. Kramer teaches us that trust can be both positive and negative:

> Human beings are naturally predisposed to trust—it's in our genes and our childhood learning—and by and large it's a survival mechanism that has served our species well. That said, our willingness to trust often gets us into trouble. Moreover, we sometimes have difficulty distinguishing trustworthy people from untrustworthy ones. At a species level, that doesn't matter very much so long as more people are trustworthy than not. At the individual level, though, it can be a real problem.[*]

As you read Kramer's words, you may be saying to yourself, "Don't I know it? Trust at the individual level can *definitely* be a real problem." My hope for you is that as you make your way through this book, you will grow in the skill of identifying whom to trust and knowing how to trust them. This way, trust will become more of a positive experience and less of a negative one. Whether your experience with trust has been good or bad, and it's likely been a mixture of both, it can be better. This is vital, because everything depends on trust.

---

[*] Roderick M. Kramer, "Rethinking Trust," *Harvard Business Review* (June 2009).

TWO

WE ARE WIRED TO TRUST

I relish my time on airplanes—those periods of quiet, alone time with no meetings and no demands. I have learned to avoid answering the common question from a seatmate: "So, what do you do?" Experience has taught me that if I say I am a psychologist, I am often in for a session I did not sign up for. But on this particular day, I slipped a bit. I was working on some research on trust, and when the man next to me asked about it, I told him. His response surprised me.

"Well, I don't trust anybody," he said. "Never have, never will. People aren't trustworthy."

"Really?" I asked. "No one? Nobody at all?"

"Absolutely not," he continued. "Trust only leads to trouble. People let you down."

"Well, I hate to tell you, but you're very mistaken about yourself," I said. "You absolutely do trust people."

"No, I don't. No way," he said. "What are you talking about?"

"You're trusting the pilot sitting in the cockpit, and you've never even met her. You trusted the guy who fueled this plane to put pure jet fuel in it instead of something else. You just ate a sandwich, trusting that the meat packer made sure it did not contain *E. coli*. You trust the mechanic who serviced the cabin compression so we have oxygen to breathe at 30,000 feet. And my hunch is that when you drove to the airport, you trusted the drivers in the opposite lane not to cross the yellow line and hit you head on. So it seems to me you have a great deal of trust. In fact, you're a pretty trusting guy."

I continued, "But what I imagine *is* true is that you don't trust people in a much more *personal* way, and that usually comes from having had some bad experiences somewhere in life. But the reality is that life itself cannot work—whether you're traveling or eating a sandwich or breathing air—without trust." I said all that, kind of wishing I hadn't, as I had just potentially entered one of those conversations I try to avoid.

As we continued talking, his story confirmed one more time how unavoidable trust is in life. At the same time, it reminded me afresh how brutally vulnerable we are when we engage in trust and it doesn't go well. This had been the case many times for the man sitting next to me before he finally gave up on trust. Or thought he had.

So, if trusting is so dangerous, why would we not be like this man? Why would we not at least stop trusting people in personal relationships or in the business arena? Why not simply try to avoid trust as much as possible? After all, it is true that trust sets us up to be disappointed or deeply hurt. It involves risk, and we can lose a lot. So why not just avoid it as much as we can?

Simply put, we *can't*, and there are good reasons for that.

We're Biologically Wired to Trust

If you have ever been around a newborn, you've noticed that newborns do not do much due diligence when they're hungry. They scream with all their might and basically say, "Bring it to me *now!*" When the breast is offered, a natural rhythm develops between a baby and a nursing mother, and it is the epitome of trust. Truly, the human infant is wired to trust. Trusting is the most natural and instinctual thing infants do. They trust first for food and then for holding and comfort. As they experience hundreds of instances of first being in distress and then consistently being delivered from the pain of hunger and aloneness by a caring person, the trust they automatically placed in Mom or a caretaker pays off and even multiplies. Trust followed by satisfaction builds more trust.

The care, comfort, and love the baby receives are gradually internalized. Neuroscience teaches us that these become actual living physical structures inside the infant's brain. Slowly an "internal mother" is neurologically constructed, and as the internal self-soothing system begins to form and develop, this will soon be able to soothe the infant from inside, even when the external mother is not present. Love actually becomes internal "equipment." Eventually, in a couple of years, this infant-turned-toddler will be able to venture into the next room and not be afraid because he will have "mommy on the inside." And one day, as an adult, this same person, now grown up, will be able to "self-regulate" his anger at a boss and keep his cool—all because a lifetime of trusting relationships produced an internalized self-soothing system.

Trust followed by satisfaction builds more trust.

Developmental psychologists call this process "developing emotional object constancy." This means that the "love object" (the caretaker) gets internalized through thousands of instances of trusting connection. At some point, an infant achieves the milestone of "secure attachment" leading to "constancy," whereby he or she feels loved even when not being attended to directly. The love is now on the inside.

As Proverbs 13:12 says, "Hope deferred makes the heart sick, but a longing fulfilled is a tree of life" (NIV). The longing for love and comfort that is fulfilled by a loving mother or primary caretaker now is a "life-giving tree" living inside, and it yields the perpetual fruit of feelings of security. This is the same process that enables terrified PTSD patients to internalize the care of a therapist and overcome the horrifying distress they have inside and, in time, realize a cure.

But no matter how loving a mother may be, if an infant does not "know" how to trust—to depend on another human being and to receive what its mother has to offer—none of her milk, love, or care will matter. The physical and emotional nourishment she offers will remain unavailable to the child if the child cannot trust. Trust makes it all happen. Without trust, the door is never opened, and nothing can get in to benefit the baby. Trust is the infant's first job, and it is a job that will not end for the rest of his or her life. And without it, the child will never know the resilient and curative effect of trust.

Since trust is so essential, it is good to know there are drugs available to help in the process! The pharmacy is right inside mother and infant in the form of powerful bonding chemicals that virtually ensure this process will take place, "gluing" them together in this bubble of safety and trust. Humans, in this case mother and child, are both chemically equipped to engage in this reciprocal relationship of trust and develop an unbreakable bond. This is part of their natural wiring. As one group of researchers put it:

> Neurobiologically oxytocin directs the young infant to preferentially select species-specific social stimuli to form dyadic attachments. . . . Increased maternal oxytocin levels were significantly related to more affectionate contact behaviors in mothers following mother-infant contact, synchrony, and engagement.

Stated more simply, *"oxytocin directs the infant to trust the mom, and vice versa."* Think about this: As human beings, our natural chemical makeup is designed to trust and to bond. We literally can't help it. God wired us this way, as Scripture attests, as a beautiful first step in even trusting Him: "You made me trust in you, even at my mother's breast" (Ps. 22:9 NIV).

**Placing our trust in other human beings
makes every system develop.**

Humans are literally wired for trust, as trust is the fuel and currency that makes all of life work, from the very beginning until the very end. Placing our trust in other human beings makes every system develop. This happens emotionally, as a child grows and develops. It happens physically, as the emotional attachment that trust brings causes brains to develop normally, immune systems to function, body weights to hit normal levels, brain sizes to achieve milestones, and on and on. It takes place socially, as the child enlarges his or her circle of trust to include more than parents and family members and ultimately includes friends and peers. Trust begets more trust. And this happens professionally, as he or she enters the world of commerce, which can only function if trust is secure. For example, if we cannot trust our markets, the entire financial system comes tumbling down, as we see when trust is leaky, such as in 2008. Trust is the most important tool we have in life, in every area. Nothing works without it.

The argument I am making here is crucial for our understanding of trust: It is *not* optional if we are going to have a good life or realize any kind of success. Period. The strategy of non-trust that my seatmate on the airplane preferred would only limit him. If you heard his story of failed relationships and businesses, you would agree. His trust issues had hindered his success in virtually every area of his life. And as the science shows us, humans do well to learn that they really are wired to live in deep, trusting relationships with others.

To Trust Is Human

You might have heard of mirror neurons. They are another example of how we are wired for trust. In the most basic terms, neurons (nerve cells) function as communicators in the body; they receive and transmit information and stimuli. Mirror neurons are at work when one person observes another person doing something and naturally imitates it. Neuroscience and fancy diagnostic equipment that allows us to see inside people's brains have taught us about mirror neurons and shown that when we feel a feeling and our body expresses it physically—in a smile or even through a miniscule muscle movement—the brain of the person we are talking to forms a connection with us and mirrors our feelings and expressions in a deep, natural bond that causes the two of us to connect even more deeply.

————

To trust is human and . . . when we can't trust, we lose a lot of the human experience.

————

When we form these deep connections, one person will even feel the feeling the other person is feeling, and this is called *empathy*, provided all is going well and that person is not unusually emotionally detached. Without going into a lot of complicated science, suffice it to say that everything we know and have learned in brain science reinforces the knowledge that humans are wired for connection. And connection is built on trust. We can basically say that to trust is human and that when we can't trust, we lose a lot of the human experience.

Love, growth, faith, physical health, economic success, and more—these all run on trust. Without trust, things stagnate or even die.

When we realize that trust is not optional, that all of human life is designed and wired to only work when we trust, we begin to treat trust with the utmost respect. And when we find that we are well-equipped to do it, we will do everything we can to make sure our trust equipment works well and can lead us to good outcomes. Trust is beneficial when it goes well, and very painful when it doesn't. Our job is to treat it with the gravitas it truly has, whether we like it or not, and to make sure trust works for us, not against us. This is precisely why, before we delve very deeply into how trust works and how to get better at it, I am working hard to help you see how deeply wired you are to trust. Because if you don't see it, it can end up hurting you.

Our strong, built-in drive to trust certainly *can* work against us. This is because everything I have mentioned about the wiring and equipment that tries to propel us to trust also pushes us toward potential danger. Almost every interaction invites us to open up, move toward, embrace, and trust other people. Our own makeup does this, and so does theirs. Yet, we know that if we do so, in many instances, we will get burned. Still, oxytocin has its way sometimes, past what our minds would have us do. Like all drugs, it can be used to heal, or to destroy.

We all have an area of the brain called the "upper brain." The upper brain is the part of the brain where the smart stuff lives—like judgment, impulse control, considering consequences, wisdom, values, and choices. The upper brain helps us know whom we can trust and whom we can't. But in some situations—when the upper brain is not being used, for example, people who form quick sexual alliances—the bonding chemicals kick in quickly with unconscious patterning and attract them to undesirable, untrustworthy people. The wiring has its way as they seductively mirror the person who wants the alliance. The wiring is that strong, and our need to trust is that strong as well.

Regardless of our particular areas of weakness and trusting too much too soon, the challenge is that our desires to trust need to have a good partnership with our objective, upper brain, which can serve as a guide as to who is trustworthy and who is not. We need our hearts and our heads to be on the same team. This is not only an issue in love or romantic relationships. We can "fall in love" and find ourselves trusting in more settings than just romance. Other desires can go awry as well, such as when you really want that business deal to go through, when you really want to be part of a certain group, or really do need to hire that new person. Ask anyone who has bought a "less-than-fully-inspected" house too quickly, made an investment unwisely, hired someone without truly vetting references, or gone into a business deal because "it sounded so great." When our desires get mixed with amped-up trust chemicals, the combination can drive us to destinations where we don't want to go. While these desires and chemicals are needed and crucial, we need both parts of our brain working together.

The takeaway here is that we humans really desire trust. We want it so much that we are always trying to move toward it unless, like the man on the plane, our experiences with broken trust have made us defensive and caused us to run away. And with such a strong drive to trust at work within us, coupled with such a strong need for it to work well, growing wiser as we grow in trust is really important. Part of the purpose of this book is to help you shape both your *desires to trust* and your *objective equipment* to help guide those desires. Remember that trust can be both positive and negative. The better your trust equipment works, the more positive your trust experiences will be.

LEARNING TO TRUST

"I can't put my finger on it. Rick is not a bad person. In fact, he's a good guy. He's smart, and he works hard. I just don't know how to describe what's wrong. We talk a lot about things we want to be different, and sometimes I think we're headed in the right direction. But before too long, something just doesn't feel right." Shannon seemed to be thinking aloud as she tried to explain to me what was wrong.

Then her husband, Colin, chimed in. "When we hired him, it was because of his experience, education, and just plain smarts. I was very impressed, and in some ways, I still am. He's interesting to talk to, but the longer a conversation goes on, the more I seem to lose some kind of 'buy in' with him. That's the only way I know how to describe it," he said.

"But it's more than that. I just can't deal with how he makes Shannon feel about the business. She and I built this company together. We've loved it for forty years, and we're overwhelmed at its success. But now, when we should be going into a season where we can coast and enjoy it, he's making it no fun at all. We seem to face one issue after another. What bothers me most is what this is doing to Shannon. She doesn't even want to come into the building anymore and that really breaks my heart. This business is our child, in a way. It's more than a family business. It really is like family to us."

"Can you help us coach Rick and get to a better place?" Colin asked. "He is so smart and capable and talented. We know he can take the business to a great place, but it just doesn't feel good right now, and this isn't how we want to live."

Colin and Shannon had built a very successful family empire, which now employed two of their adult children. They had made great plans for the next generation to take over, but they needed a CEO in the interim. They hired Rick for this position, thinking he would lead the company for about ten years, until one of their children would be ready to take the helm. But as they kept talking, I concluded that everything might be up for grabs.

Colin and Shannon had hired me to provide CEO coaching with Rick and to do some team building with his executive team because a few VPs were not happy with the culture he was forming and the way things were going. This was our first meeting and I wanted to get the story from them before I met Rick the following day.

As I continued to listen, the breach between them and Rick seemed to grow. They spoke of several times they simply did not connect with him or the way he ran the company. Nothing overtly ugly was happening—no embezzlement or bullying or bad decisions on his part. In fact, most decisions he made actually made good business sense. Something else was going on, something that had nothing to do with actual bad behavior.

But the more Colin and Shannon shared, the more I knew exactly what the problem was.

"I'd like you guys to do something," I said. "I am going to ask you five questions about Rick. I want you to take some time apart from each other and think about them separately. Then, rate Rick from 1 to 5 on each of the questions. When you are finished, we'll resume. Got it?"

"Sure . . . I think," said Colin. "What are the questions?"

"Get a pad of paper and write these down," I said. I went to the white board and wrote the questions where they could see them:

1. How much do you feel Rick truly, deeply understands what you need and want in the business and how you feel about those things? How well is he able to communicate that to you?
2. How much do you feel his motive—his ongoing intent—is to do what you desire *for* the business and *with* the business versus what he might want and desire for the company or even for himself?
3. How capable do you feel he is of delivering what you want him to deliver and build?
4. How much do you feel he exhibits the personal and interpersonal traits you need him to show toward you and with his team? How much is his "makeup" what you need for what you want?
5. How is he building a track record that causes you to expect good things will happen tomorrow and in the future?

Colin and Shannon stared at the questions intently. After a few minutes, I noticed engagement building as they read over them. That showed something was happening inside them. They were already processing. The questions were doing their work.

They each went to their own space. As they did their thinking, I went to get some coffee and walked around the executive floor, looking at the various awards the company had won, pictures of people and milestones, and photos of happy times and celebrations, going back to their first small office building. It was obvious this company was a good place and had been for a long time. I was saddened to see how different the gallery of the company's history looked compared to what I had heard from the founders that morning.

After about twenty minutes, I saw Colin and Shannon walk back into the beautiful glass-walled boardroom overlooking the Pacific Ocean. I followed them in.

"So, let me see your numbers," I began.

When they handed me their answers, I was surprised on one level. Yet on another level, I was not surprised at all. Their ratings all hovered around 2 on the scale of 1 to 5.

I had my answer.

"I think I know what's wrong," I said.

"What?" Shannon asked.

"You don't trust him," I answered.

Silence. They initially looked puzzled, but then turned to each other and stared. Then they turned to me and Shannon spoke first.

"That's exactly right! I *don't* trust him. But I'm confused. I never thought about our difficulties with Rick being about *trust*. I mean, I don't think he would ever lie or cheat or steal or anything like that. He is very moral, very ethical. It doesn't seem like a matter of trust, but for some reason, you're right. I just don't trust him."

Then Colin said, "I feel the same way. He is a really honest, stand-up guy. But I don't feel like I trust him either. How can this be? How can someone have good character, but you still don't feel like you trust him?"

"Happens all the time," I offered. "Trust goes far beyond honesty or ethics. It's about much more than knowing whether or not someone will lie to you. Trust is the confidence that someone will guard what is important to you, what you need, possess, or desire. Whatever your interests are, someone you trust will safeguard the interests you entrust to them.

"You may entrust many kinds of interests to people—emotional, business, physical, financial, spiritual, and others. Even if that person is ethical, you need more than ethics from someone you trust. It is also vital that you feel they will guard and care about your interests and be able to take care of them well. They can have integrity in all kinds of ways, but they can still prove untrustworthy by not coming through in the ways you are trusting them to come through for you.

"Think of an honest husband whose wife cannot trust him to respond to her emotional needs or an honest boss whose employees do not trust to take them seriously or respond well when they go to him with a problem. Think of an honest team member who doesn't perform well. There are different kinds of trust in different kinds of relationships for different needs. To feel safe, certain factors besides honesty and morality must be present in the relationship.

"In terms of what you need from Rick as CEO of your company, I don't get the impression you can trust him to provide what you need. And your greatest need is not to have to worry about the business."

"I can't tell you how many lights are coming on right now," Colin said. "I'd describe it all as a kind of 'worry.' I would never be concerned about Rick stealing, but I haven't been able to stop worrying about the company since he's been running it. I keep wondering where it will be in a few years and what it will feel like. I find myself worrying a lot, but I can't put my finger on why."

"Well, let me help you," I said. "Look at the questions. Take the first one, for example. For you to trust that someone will do what you need in a relationship, you have to feel they really make an effort to listen and *understand* your needs. *You need to feel that they know what it feels like to be you in whatever you are doing.* You and Shannon both rated him low on that question. If he doesn't try to get to know what matters to you, you end up feeling not understood and a little queasy. You can't just let go of it and not worry."

"I always feel that way with him," said Colin. "When you use the word *listen,* it makes more sense. When I wanted a deep discussion about the company's DNA and what matters to me, he'd start talking to me about all the ways he understands and drives DNA as a leader.

He talked about how much he 'gets it,' but didn't seem to hear how I saw it and what I wanted. I felt a little ignored—or invisible. Is that what you mean?"

"Exactly," I said. "It sounds like he was persuading you more than he was listening to understand your needs and desires for the company. So, deep inside, you recognized at some level that you were not really 'known.' Not feeling known creates the sense that you can't trust someone because you realize they don't really know or 'get' what matters to you. So, you never can really 'let go.'

"In fact, *letting go* is a good term because it gets to the feeling I like to use when talking about trust, and that feeling is *carelessness*," I said.

"Careless? Why would I want to be careless," Colin asked. "This is our business. We would never be careless with it."

"I didn't say be careless with your business. What I mean is that your confidence in Rick should be so high that you don't have to feel you are always 'on guard' about the business or worrying about it. You can be 'careless' in the sense of not having to 'take care' of yourself. When we trust someone, we can forget about having to watch our back or watch out for whatever we have entrusted to them. We feel we don't have a care in the world about it because that person will take care of everything.

"This kind of carelessness is much different than being careless about your business. In fact, it is caring so much that you put the right steward in charge of it, someone that will take the same care of it that you would, so you don't have to worry.

"For example, in the last thirty minutes, how much have you worried about your money in your checking account? Zero, right? You have been pretty 'careless' about it, I would say. I haven't seen you check your balance one time. Why? Because you know that the bank is taking care of guarding it. They have alarm systems, security, managers, regulators, and lots of ways to 'care' about it so that you don't have to. This is what I mean by 'careless.' Someone else, someone you trust, is caring so you don't have to. That's why you hire a CEO—so you can be 'careless.'"

"This makes sense," Colin said. Shannon added, "I am tired of being concerned about where the company is going. As you've explained it, our problem really is about trust. We need to be able to trust him, and we don't."

"We've only discussed the first of the five questions. I think if we went through all of them, you would even see more reasons you feel this way and be more convinced of what I think will be the answer to your problem," I interjected.

"I think I know what our solution is," Shannon said, looking at Colin. His nod said all I needed to know about what they were thinking.

"The thing is that we just never have been able to wrap our heads around what it was, what was underneath what we were feeling," she continued. "He works so hard, and is so good at what he does. It was just so confusing. He is so competent—and even charming. Now, the issue is so clear. It's *trust*.

"There was always a situation," she said. "For example, he would come up with ideas other people would think were great, but they were not 'us.' Or, he would pursue relationships with the types of companies we wouldn't normally align with. They would be good businesses, just not who we are. His moves looked good on paper, but many of them just didn't feel right. There were many incidents I never rolled into a single issue like trust. But you're right, I never felt I could just let go without worrying or trying to take care of things."

"Without fully going into it, when you think of question two, about 'motive,' or 'intent,' I bet his motive was really about what he wanted the company to be—his vision, more than yours," I hypothesized.

"Yes, it *felt* that way. This is *our* company," Colin said. "But we slowly felt it might be becoming something other than what we had built and wanted. Now that we are talking about it, it was gradually going to turn into *Rick's* company, not ours. I wanted him to *run it,* not *change it.* I think his intent was more about his interests than ours. I hadn't thought about it in these terms until now."

For the remainder of that day, Colin, Shannon, and I talked some more and unpacked their feelings in each dimension. I wanted them to be sure of the decision they had made so quickly. But by the end of the day, they had canceled the next day with Rick. They had some other meetings to take care of—with their attorneys and human resources people—to plan Rick's exit. Once some clarity had been found, the path had emerged.

Clarity Can Lead *to* Trust or Protect You *from* Trusting

What happened for Shannon and Colin as they worked through the five questions helped them clearly see the problem in their business. The clarity they gained can also happen *before* one hires someone like Rick, if that person knows what to look and listen for. If you have already engaged someone, as they had, you can often correct the problem if you know what to look for to evaluate trust and build it. Many times you can make attempts to correct it and succeed. If not, you can then know that it is time for a necessary ending of the relationship.

Trust is much easier to build, enter into, avoid, or
repair if we know what to look for.

But it takes an awareness of what to examine in a relationship to know what to address and try to correct or eliminate. That's what the questions were designed to do, and these questions are about the dynamics that we will examine in the rest of this book. The dynamics we'll look at come together to provide a model of trust that your "thinking brain" can use when the rest of you says "go." It'll either confirm your "go," tell you to stop, or perhaps tell you that feeling like you want to say "no" could be rooted in some fear or issue inside of you more than in a real reason to not trust someone. The basic idea is this: *trust is much easier to build, enter into, avoid, or repair if we know what to look for.*

Knowing what to look for helps equip us in contexts beyond hiring and personnel issues as well:

- A single person deciding whether someone is relationship potential
- A married person trying to identify the *real* problem in their relationship
- A company trying to address a concern with a vendor, a supplier, or even an employee
- A parent setting boundaries with a child or teen or talking to them about a behavior problem
- A business knowing what to address in their products, services, people, or messaging in order to build trust with customers and potential customers
- An entrepreneur gaining the trust of investors
- A wife being able to sleep soundly while her husband is traveling, feeling quite "careless" while he is a thousand miles away
- A leader knowing how to build trust among his or her team
- A medical facility being able to build trust with patients and a community
- A church developing trust with the community it serves
- A salesperson trying to serve a customer or gain a sale
- A customer service representative turning an angry caller into a raving fan
- A nonprofit organization building trust with donors

You may be thinking of circumstances in your life that aren't on my list above. You feel confused because you don't know exactly what's wrong, but you're certain something isn't right. The five crucial issues that help us know whether to move forward or to pull away apply to every scenario I can think of, so let's recap them briefly here before diving deeply into them in the next section of this book. They are the same five that helped Shannon and Colin gain immediate clarity and serve as the model for this book:

1. *You can trust someone when you feel your needs are understood, felt, and cared about.*

   People are often too self-centered to even see what you need and what matters to you. It may be that their own needs are more important to them than yours or that they have their own agenda, sometimes even selfish or destructive. Until you feel understood and believe someone really gets what matters to you, what hurts you, and what makes you feel good, trust will be low. If they haven't listened enough and communicated to you their accurate understanding of you and your needs, trust suffers. It will be difficult to be "careless."

2. *You can trust someone when you feel their motive is for you, not just for themselves.*

   A relationship you can trust is one that has your back. While people have their own interests to pursue and guard, people you trust will look out for yours as well. They will do nothing to harm you. While they might have to say no to you sometimes, they always sincerely want the best for you. Beyond that, when in their power, even in your absence, they will do what is best for you, even at times to their own loss, or cost. They are "for" you.

3. *You can trust someone when you feel they have the ability or capacity to guard and deliver results for what you have entrusted to them.* Someone might be understanding of what you need and care about, and they may want the best for you, yet may not have the skills to do what you need them to do in the relationship. These may be professional abilities or personal competencies. For us to feel "careless," we have to know our needs will be adequately taken care of in the ways that we have trusted someone to do. That person has to be able to pull it off. Deliver on the promise.

4. *You can trust someone who has the character or personal makeup needed for what you entrust them with.* Character begins with foundational traits such as honesty, faithfulness, and integrity. Without these qualities, there can be no trust; they are "permission to play" traits. But much more is needed to trust someone in certain relationships or contexts. While compassion may be needed in one context, courage or perseverance may be needed in another where compassion is not. Open-mindedness may be valuable in one arena, while fidelity to specific policies or standards could be vital in another. The character traits needed to trust will vary, but character is always a factor. Personal makeup matters.

5. *You can trust someone who has a track record of performing in the ways you need them to perform.* Our minds build maps to know how to negotiate the world. You can trust that if you go down your stairs and turn right, the kitchen will be there, because it was there yesterday. Similarly, track records build maps. When someone delivers upon a promise or meets a need in a certain way repeatedly, we trust more deeply. When a track record is broken or a pattern of

setbacks occurs, trust wanes or is destroyed. You will depend on someone based on what happened last time you trusted them. Behavior builds expectations, either good or bad. Trustworthy or untrustworthy.

As we go forward, we will look thoroughly into and examine the five essentials of trust: understanding, motive, ability, character, and track record. We'll explore the traits, behaviors, skills, and attitudes that bring them to reality and enable them to be felt, experienced, and lived out in our relationships and in every area of our lives. The more we can identify and understand these traits, the better we can perceive them in others and live them out ourselves. This knowledge will help us to know what to look for in other people as we decide whom to trust, leading us to more trusting relationships and giving us greater ability to avoid people and situations that will bring us harm.

THE FIVE ESSENTIALS OF TRUST

FOUR

UNDERSTANDING: THE FIRST ESSENTIAL OF TRUST

You are an FBI hostage negotiator and you're needed immediately. A bomber has taken twenty-four customers captive in a bank in downtown Chicago and issued his demands. The police have made contact and told him they were sending someone in to talk to him about what he wants and how they will get it to him. That person is you. What do you do?

If you think the way most people think, you know exactly what you would say: "What are you thinking, Jason? This is stupid and it won't end well. There's no way out of this place, and you are going to end up dead. Just take off the vest and do the right thing so this goes in a good direction."

Leading someone to trust you does not begin with convincing them that you are right.

You *know* what is right. You *know* what is smart, at least in the way that you or most intelligent people would think about it. So you know your job is to get the bomber to trust your way of thinking, listen to your persuasive logic, agree with your solution, and march right out of the bank. You'll convince him of the smart thing to do and he'll do it. You think that *persuasion* is the best strategy. Right? You have to get him to see the light.

No.

Not if you understand the dynamics of trust. In fact, if you really were a hostage negotiator and reviewed the above script, you'd probably hear explosions in your head as you read it. Why? Because you know better than to try to get someone to trust you by talking them into it. You know the dynamics of trust, and you realize that leading someone to trust you does not begin with convincing them that you are right. In fact, it doesn't begin with convincing them of *anything* you are thinking. It doesn't begin with persuasion, logic, facts, or intelligent, airtight arguments that will make them realize that you know better. Trust doesn't start with convincing someone that you are right, or smart, or even trustworthy.

It begins with helping someone to know that you understand them.

Where Trust Begins

The process of trust begins by *listening* and by understanding other people—what they want and what they're feeling—in short, knowing what matters to them. *The task is to know them instead of to persuade them*. People *must* feel known in order to trust. Trust begins not with convincing someone to trust you; it starts with someone feeling that you *know* them.

As a real FBI hostage negotiator, Chris Voss, puts it: "As I've worked with executives and students to develop these skills, I always try to reinforce the message that *being right isn't the key to a successful negotiation—having the right mindset is*."[*] The mindset to which

---

[*] Chris Voss and Tahl Raz, *Never Split the Difference* (New York: HarperCollins, 2016), 43. Kindle edition.

Voss refers is one of deep *empathy*—listening to understand the other person and *having that person understand that you understand.*

When someone feels that you understand them, something magical happens. The brain begins to change, to move from its neutral or guarded state, or an "against you" state, to an *open* state. Their brain opens up to being open to you, and trust takes its first step. This is physical and chemical, as well as psychological and spiritual.

———

**Trust begins not with convincing someone
to trust you; it starts with someone feeling
that you *know* them.**

———

Brain science teaches us that we are designed to begin to open ourselves to trusting someone when we feel they understand us, when we feel *mirrored* by them. A mirror reflects back to us who we are, and in the deepest communications between people, reflecting back to someone who they are says: "I see you. I hear you. I know who you are." This opens their heart to feeling safe.

A great example of this is when a mother and an infant engage in the mirroring dance. As the mother reflects the baby's expressions back to him or her, the basis for connection builds. Oxycontin begins flowing, and the bonds develop. This is the dance of *mirroring.* Mirroring is basically what it says it is. It is mirroring back to the person what he or she tells you so that it says, "I get you. I really hear you." As that happens, the brain shifts gears. The suspicious or closed-off brain that is driven by fear begins to shut down and the upper brain gets engaged. When we feel understood, fear and resistance calm down and we open up. We can listen better, think better, reason better, use better judgment, and have a potentially productive conversation. This all begins by being understood. Mirror neurons have done their work and led to communication and connection.

Apply this to the hostage situation. Instead of the negotiator saying, "Take off the vest, put the bomb down, and let's do the smart thing," the negotiator takes a different approach. "Hi. I'm Josh and they sent me up here to understand what's going on. What's your name?"

"David."

"Hi, David. What's going on? Tell me how we got here today."

With this approach, a slow dance unfolds. The hostage taker gradually reveals a little more about who he is, what has happened, and how he has come to this moment. And as all of that is happening, a little window of trust is opening up. A window where a dialogue is building that will allow the negotiator to find a solution acceptable to the hostage taker and avert the crisis. The dance has built trust. It is an investment *in* the relationship.

This dance is the dance of *mirroring*. As that happens, the brain shifts gears. The suspicious or closed-off brain that is driven by fear begins to shut down and the upper brain gets engaged. When we feel understood, that understanding calms down fear and resistance and we open up. We can actually listen better ourselves, think better, reason better, use better judgment, and have a conversation that can go somewhere productive. And it all begins by being understood.

Think about our story in chapter 1. The chairman was done. His brain had shut down the possibility of trust. He was literally and figuratively "out the door."

But when I asked him how he felt when the CEO treated him dismissively, he cracked just a little. Someone had actually wanted to "know him," what his experience was like. My question showed him that, unlike the CEO, someone wanted to hear what being in that relationship was like for him. I was interested in what *he* was thinking and feeling. That little question that said, "I am interested in knowing you," caused him pause. It opened him up just enough to feel something, as first evidenced by his quivering jaw. As he spoke, I simply nodded and mirrored back a few words: "It's horrible to feel that way. You must feel so dismissed when he does that." As I did, and he began disclosing more, the CEO could finally see him and see what he had unwittingly done to him.

The CEO's human compassion kicked in, and that is when he came over and said he was sorry and he would "never want to make him feel that way." His message was: "I see you and understand what I have put you through. I'm sorry for that and I want something different." Then, we had something to build on, and the two reached a resolution.

Part of the prayer attributed to St. Francis of Assisi says, "Grant that I may not so much seek . . . to be understood, as to understand." This is actually great brain science. "Telling" does little good if no one is listening. And people begin to listen after feeling like they have been listened to. From big time corporate leaders to hostage takers to five-year-olds, we all want to be known and understood before we take input.

My friend, a psychologist, was single parenting for a week while his wife was on a trip to see her parents. One morning as it was time to get going for the day, and after telling his six-year-old to get ready to go, he came back into her room only to find her lollygagging and doing nothing that approached getting ready to leave.

"Millie," he pushed. "I told you we have to go. Get your shoes on and be ready to get into the car. We have to leave or we are going to be late." He went to do something else, and when he returned a few minutes later, she had made zero progress toward being ready to leave.

Growing frustrated, he raised his voice and said, "Millie! I told you we have to leave, and you are not getting ready. Now come on!"

She began crying and turned away from him. He first felt more frustration, but then he stopped.

"I asked myself," he told me, "if this were one of my patients, what would I do? Then it hit me."

He walked over to her, sat down, put his arm around her, looked her in the eye, and said, "You miss your mommy, don't you?"

Immediately she broke down crying, fell into his arms, and just sobbed.

"I miss her too," he said. "I miss her too."

She cried for a few more minutes, and then suddenly jumped up and said, "Daddy! We have to hurry! We have to get to school!"

What happened there? The same dynamic that made a chairman of the board and a CEO able to trust each other and to work together again. The same dynamic an FBI negotiator experiences in a successful hostage situation. The same dynamic successful marriages experience, especially in moments of significant conflict. The same dynamic parents who do well with teenagers have in their relationship with that half-child/half-adult. And the same dynamic successful companies and organizations have with their customers and stakeholders: Trust built through someone feeling understood. Trust that allows us to know that "this person knows me. This person knows what I am feeling, what I want, what matters to me," and more.

Understanding Is More Than Listening

Early in psychotherapy research, Carl Rogers proved he could get clinical results by *only* listening and listening in a way that mirrored the patient's experience so they felt "heard." This has now been proven in settings beyond psychotherapy—in marriage and parenting, business teams, leadership, medicine, sales, customer service, and other areas.

The other day, a friend of mine who had bought a new car had something go wrong with the door and called the dealership to tell them about the problem. The service department was familiar with the problem, based on the complaints of other owners of that model, and said they would send someone out to his house to fix it. That surprised him for sure, but what really surprised him was how understood he felt by the mechanic who came and fixed it. The mechanic looked at the door and said, "This is terrible. This should never have happened to you! What a pain for you to have to deal with this after buying a new car! I'll get it fixed, but I am really sorry this happened."

My friend was grateful that his car was fixed, but even more powerful was the mechanic's empathy for and understanding of what he had felt. Not that a broken door on a car is the same as many more horrible things that can happen to us in life—it is kind of trivial in the big picture. But, the fact that he felt understood in a very small thing is somewhat evidence of how powerful feeling understood is in general. Experience of feeling understood sticks with us. Think of the trust my friend has for that company now. And think about the trust created in much weightier issues of life if people feel like someone finally understands, someone finally "gets it." Breakthroughs can happen.

Feeling understood goes way past just listening. Listening is only the beginning, an interpersonal skill that leads to and enhances the feeling of being understood. But truly being understood in the way that leads to trust is when someone acts on their understanding in ways that prove to the person, "Wow. You really do get me. You really do know what I need." By listening, one gains true knowledge of the other. That knowledge is further felt through affecting someone's actions. The rest of this book will go into much detail about the kinds of actions that prove that the listening was correct. But the point here is this:

> We can never act in ways that cause someone to trust us if we do not understand what they feel, think, need, desire, and fear.

As one of my favorite verses says:

One who gives an answer before he hears, it is foolishness and
shame to him. —Proverbs 18:13 NASB

The Hebrew word for "hears," *Shama*, can also be translated as understands (Strong's Concordance 8085).

There are many, many times when attempts to give someone the answer we think they need fail because it is so far from who they really are and what they truly desire and need. Ask any spouse who has truly felt like they loved their spouse, only to come home to a note that says "I am leaving. It's over." They wonder what happened, as in their mind they were doing a good job of "loving." But it was never love based on real understanding, the only basis for truth.

Let's go back to Colin and Shannon. Rick failed at listening in some critical ways and never truly understood what *they* wanted for the business. He was more interested in telling them what *he* could do for the business. I can just hear him even though I never met him, for I have met him a thousand times with a thousand different names. He is the person who when you are trying to share something important, it only becomes a cue to instantly talk about his views, life, or something personal. And that is the essence of this aspect of the breakdown of trust:

When we fail to understand someone at a deep level, we unknowingly communicate that we are only interested in ourselves.

Rick would certainly not have said that, nor did he probably believe it. From all Shannon and Colin said, he cared about them and the company. But he cared about them in the way *he* thought about caring for them. *His* way, *his* opinions, *his* methods, and the like. That does not lead to anyone feeling understood. In fact, it only leads them to feel more alone and shut down, the opposites of trust.

In being a persuader instead of a listener, Rick lost Shannon and Colin. He was hired to lead *their* company with *their* ways, using his talents. But he never really knew what their company was. He was leading another company than the one he was hired to lead. Without realizing it, he made his job all about him and very little about them. That was the first breach of trust that he committed.

Every day, bosses, parents, spouses, doctors, politicians, and others do the same thing. *Being able to see this when this is happening to you is critical to knowing whom to trust.*

Consider these examples:

- You explain to your boss why something isn't working, and he doesn't hear you. He just keeps telling you why it should work just fine, and to keep doing it his way.
- You try to get your spouse to see how she is hurting you or how you feel sometimes in the relationship, and she negates what you are saying.
- You spend time with someone you are dating whom you find very attractive or charming, yet afterward he knows very little about you and you feel "alone."
- You try to explain your symptoms to your doctor, but she rushes through the exam seeming to already have an answer in her head, and you feel "missed."
- You try to communicate to your business partner that he isn't pulling his weight, but he can't hear how you feel like you are doing the work of two people.
- You call a customer service line, and after explaining the problem three times, she keeps giving you the same answer, saying, "Well, if you do this, it 'should work.'"
- You are going through something significant and share it with a friend, who immediately just tells you what to do or, worse, says, "Oh, I know. When that happened to me . . ."

Compare those with these:

- A boss who says, "I understand that what I gave you to do isn't working. That's got to be frustrating. Help me understand where the obstacle is. Tell me how what I thought isn't the right fit so I can understand and help you find the right one."
- Your spouse says, "So you feel like I am more attentive to my work and friends than to you, like they come first and you feel alone a lot, like you don't matter to me as much as they do. That's horrible."
- Your date says, "You said earlier that you moved here because things had gotten difficult back home. What was happening? What was it like back there? Sounds like it must have been pretty difficult if it made you move across the country."
- Your doctor says, "Let me make sure I am getting it. Sometimes the pain starts slowly and builds and other times it just comes on all at once, and you've been experiencing it how long?"
- Your business partner says, "So you feel like you are doing way too much and that I'm letting you down, like I'm not doing my share?"
- The customer service representative says, "It's frustrating when you do everything the instructions tell you to do, and you do it right, and it still won't work. Let's figure out what's going on."
- Your friend says, "Wow, that must have been really hard when he did that, like all that work you did didn't even matter."

You can feel the difference between the simple statements in the first list and the ones in the second list. The key is that we can go somewhere productive when we have been heard. We know better what people need, what the real issues are, or aren't. Sometimes, listening is all people want anyway and nothing more is needed. Few things are more frustrating than not being heard when something is important to us.

But lest we think that just "hearing" and "mirroring" are all that are needed in this aspect of trust, remember that we need to be heard for other reasons besides being known. As we have seen, the first is to establish the connection, to begin to build the trust bond that starts with being known. This is the glue that begins to give the relationship stability. But to build trust, we need also to be heard so the person knows what we need and can meet that need in the relationship.

When we know someone, we learn what they like, what they need, and what they desire, and very importantly, we learn what hurts them. We can then put that knowledge into actions that meet their needs and that avoid causing them pain.

Had Rick simply listened to Colin and Shannon and really understood all that was important to them about the continuity of the identity of the company, he could have suggested a company-wide meeting where he interviewed them about the values and DNA of the organization and let them talk about how those values could be lived out in the future. He could have requested regular meetings so they could give him feedback on his performance through the transition. He could have invited them on visits to manufacturers and distributors, to learn from how they interacted with them.

I think, had Rick approached Colin and Shannon this way, they would have felt much more understood. Then trust would have been a real possibility. This type of approach would have demonstrated his desire to understand them, and he would have followed up with actions.

Understanding Is More Than Relational

Understanding isn't limited to interpersonal relationships. Businesses and organizations can also endeavor to understand the needs and desires of their customers and members. For example, I prefer a certain hotel chain over all others when I travel for business. While it has many features and amenities other chains have, there's something different about this one. And surprisingly, it is not the most expensive hotel in its category. But if I have the option, I'll choose it over the more expensive ones. The reason? I feel like they get me. They understand me. I don't know how they did it, maybe through a zillion customer surveys, interviews, or a CEO who spent a hundred nights a year in them, but they do get it.

It's little things that make these places work for me. They've thought through the questions that are important to me. Are the charger outlets accessible and not stuck behind the bed where you need an excavation crew to get to them? Are there work spaces that you can actually do work in? Are the conference spaces I may need for work or a meeting conveniently located? What kind of coffee setup is in the room and how well stocked is it? What food offerings are available at the times business travelers actually need to eat? Does someone answer the phone promptly when you dial the front desk? Are the irons clean, not covered with burned starch from the last guy's clothes that will ruin mine? Are the shampoo and body wash bottles readable without a microscope, and do they have enough of them? Are the pillows less than four stories thick?

I could go on with my personal rant, but in many hotels I often ask myself, "Has the person who owns this place actually ever stayed in it? Does he understand anything about what people need? Give me the cheap hotel where I feel understood!"

Great businesses are built on a deep, empathic relationship with customers.

Great businesses are built on a deep, empathic relationship with customers. They *understand* their customers. They *know* them. And if they understand and know them, they can make them happy and taken care of. As a result, the next time the customer books a trip, she says to the travel department of her company, "Make sure you book me in the X." Why? Simply trust. She can trust that they have her back and she is careless about her lodging once she knows where she is staying. Not another thought.

Chick-fil-A is a great company, and I've had the privilege of working with them for a long time. They certainly have "trust" with all the customers that love them. The reasons for this are many, and one of them is that Chick-fil-A goes to great lengths to make sure they understand their customers' needs and follow up with actions that meet those needs. They think about this a lot. Here's my favorite example.

Consider this: You are an overtaxed mom and you have loaded your three kids—ages 2, 5, and 7—in the minivan to grab some food on the way home from the doctor's office. On the way to Chick-fil-A, it starts *pouring down raining*. All you can think about is how you will get the kids out of car seats and into the restaurant without getting drenched. You pray the rain lets up before you get there.

But it doesn't. You sit for a moment in the parking lot, in the downpour. You could go through the drive-through, but you really want to get it all done with a sit-down meal. Suddenly, someone knocks at your window. It's the owner-operator and another employee with two golf umbrellas there to escort you and your kids into the store, completely dry.

This may seem too good to be true. But it happens. You feel *so* understood—like they know exactly what your life is like and what you need—that your trust in them is forever solidified. It goes through the roof.

Not only is this a great example of empathic actions—meaning actions based on truly understanding what someone needs—it is an even greater example of a company culture building and gaining trust through every action, from the way they treat their employees to the mom in the rain. They spend significant focused time thinking about what the customer's experience is actually like and identifying where they can jump into that experience to meet the needs they come to understand. This creates "raving fans," as Ken Blanchard says.

There's more to the Chick-fil-A philosophy. Otherwise, empathy would be only a technique, a tool. But they really care about it. Their corporate purpose includes having "a positive influence on all who come in contact with Chick-fil-A." It is genuine, from the top down, a family owned and run business for three generations that has built a legacy of serving others. They look to hire people who want to be in the "serving others business," and they have chosen the restaurant industry as the place they get to do it. Their understanding, help, and care are real—and very fruitful for both their customers and them.

For empathy to affect trust, it must be real. It can't be scripted, like many cheesy customer service calls. We have to truly care. But, we can really care and still fail to understand what someone feels or needs from us. We can care deeply, yet not be able to truly see and understand someone else's experience. Empathy comes from putting ourselves in someone else's situation and identifying with their experience.

This all comes from a biblical value of love, as expressed through the Golden Rule:

Treat others as you would want to be treated.

If you're a busy mom, you would want some help with three little kids in the rain, right? So, treat a mom like you would want to be treated. The Golden Rule is based on empathy, on understanding another person—his or her situation, needs, desires, wishes, and pains—then meeting those needs the way you'd want someone to meet yours if it were you.

I don't know who first asked the moms about dealing with rain and parking lots. But I do know someone at Chick-fil-A at least asked themselves, "What would I do for that mom if I really understood her daily burdens? What would deep understanding look like at our restaurant?" Then someone went and figured it out.

I love the story of how Saddleback Church was founded. Before Rick Warren launched the church, his team phoned and knocked on doors throughout Saddleback Valley to ask people one question: "Do you go to church?"

If the person said "yes," they said, "Great. God bless you and have a nice day." But, if the answer was "no," they immediately followed up with, "Why not?"

They gathered those answers, the real reasons people did not go to church, and took them to their planning room. They then began to plan a church that *would have none of those reasons*. They removed the things that people don't want, don't like, get hurt by, or don't meet people's real needs and built a church based on understanding what people truly need and want.

Forty years later, tens of thousands of people attend Saddleback Church each week. This is what happens when you truly listen and understand.

What if:

- A husband really understood what his detachment from the family felt like to his wife and children
- An alcoholic deeply heard and felt what her drinking was doing to her loved ones and business partners
- A critical spouse really understood what happens in the heart of the one criticized or screamed at

- A boss really knew what it feels like for his employee to be shamed in front of the rest of the team
- The doctor knew what it did to someone's day to take off work for a 2:30 appointment, arrive at 2:30, and not be seen until 3:55
- An airline understood what it feels like to have your plane canceled at the last minute on your way to an important life event

So there is our first building block of trust, being and feeling understood, whether it happens in relationships between individuals or in groups, or in some kind of business or consumer setting. Understanding has emotional, psychological, physical, and communication components. It is a lifelong skill that begins in infancy and develops throughout our lives as we grow more in being connected to others and their experiences.

Figuring out when we ourselves are understood and when we are not is also a lifelong skill. It takes a lot of wisdom, as we are wired to need it and people can fake it well. We all know the experience of meeting someone and feeling so "connected" very quickly, only to find out there are real monsters lurking in that person's trunk. It takes time to reveal who people really are, and we'll examine those diagnostic skills later in the book. For now, just start noticing the people you feel really get you, understand you, and know what you experience. Notice the ones with whom you feel safe. Learning to know when trust is available is a great skill to hone. But as good as it is, it can be misleading or insufficient. It is possible for someone to understand you well, and still not be a person you should trust. That's why it's important to look at the other essentials of trust.

FIVE

MOTIVE:
THE SECOND ESSENTIAL OF TRUST

A few years ago, I began having some serious knee pain. I had always had bad knees from sports and sports-related injuries, motorcycle crashes, and skiing mishaps, but it was getting worse. I had one surgery many years ago and hoped I would be able to stave off needing another one, even though the surgeon then told me I was not looking good long-term.

I did not want a total knee replacement. I had friends who had been through it, and they said it was an awful experience. One close friend had to have his redone three times because he had an infection and some other complications. Having had enough surgeries for several people, I was not eager to go through with this "internal amputation," as one surgeon called it. So I put it off.

But when I reached the point that I could no longer walk after I hit the pavement on Santa Monica Pier one day, and ended up in the emergency room, it was time to see a surgeon. I had to find the right doctor.

I did my research and went to see the first highly recommended orthopedic surgeon. The nurse led me into the exam room, and after a little while, he came in. After introducing himself, he said, "Lie down and let me feel that leg." He did a stability exam, bending it this way and that, pushing here and there. After what seemed like about two or three minutes, he said, "Yeah. I looked at your X-rays and I know what's going on. You need a total knee replacement. There is no other surgery that is going to help this, so that's what you need. Let us know if that is what you want to do." And he began to walk out.

I stopped him. "Dr. . . . I have a question."

"Yes?" he asked.

"Uhm . . . that is kind of a big deal. Don't you need an MRI or something? Can you really tell me that after a couple of minutes and just feeling around? A total knee?"

"Actually, I can. That is how we diagnose it along with the pain picture you have. I totally understand what your problem is and a replacement is what you need. Anyone that tells you differently is just wrong. This is what I do," he answered. And with that, he left. A few minutes interaction to plan my future of walking.

I sat there and was a bit caught between two feelings. One was, "Oh, crap. It's true. I have to have my knee replaced. They told me it would likely come to this." But then there was another feeling: "I just don't feel good about him. Everybody said he's great, but I just don't feel sure. It just doesn't feel right."

While he said he understood what was going on with my knee, somehow I did not feel understood. Somehow trust was still lacking. Plus, he seemed a little more interested in getting to his next whatever than tending to me.

I wanted another opinion and kept looking.

After more searches, another name kept coming up and I went to see him, the department head at a great teaching hospital. He talked a lot about his work in knee replacements, himself, and all about what he did. And he had students in the room with me the whole time showing them what *he* did. I felt a little like a cadaver they use in medical school. They also sent a few students in to do random things to my leg so they could gain some experience. Nothing wrong with that—I was a doctoral student once too. But, somehow, the whole thing seemed a little more about his expert teaching agenda, audience, and all the great things he did than about my inability to walk or go through a day without excruciating pain.

We ended that visit with his diagnosis: "You need a total knee replacement. I understand what's happening here. There's no doubt that is what you need. Let us know when you want to do it." And he walked out. As he was leaving, he immediately immersed himself in reviewing the exam with his students. He was onstage again.

I checked out, and as I drove home, I had the same uneasiness. I just was not feeling like I had found the right one.

It was clear that both surgeons "understood" me in terms of truly understanding my medical issues. However, they both could have done a lot better on the emotional connection and empathic understanding that I needed, as we just reviewed. Even though they had the skill to help me, something was missing. And as I was about to realize, there was more missing than just the emotional understanding. There was also something else.

Later, after I left, I figured out what was missing: What was missing in this picture was *me*.

I was missing. I was nowhere in the picture of what they cared about, it seemed. While they understood me and what I needed, it felt like everything was all about them and not about me. And I was the patient. My "trust" button was not getting pushed. It seemed like they were motived by their agendas, schedules, and priorities more than motivated to help me.

I then went back and read all of the patient reviews about these two great surgeons, and the reviews said pretty much what I was feeling. About the first one, even though he was regarded as a genius, they said that when they were there, he seemed to just be about *his* schedule, *his* demands, *his* this and that. They described the office as feeling like the whole scene was set up around *him* and *his* universe, not about the patient. It was more like an assembly line from the patient's perspective.

And with the second one, it was all about not only him, but his teaching agenda. He passed the first trust ingredient in that I felt like he "understood" my need (at least medically), but I felt a bit like I had been a textbook or a plastic model instead of a patient. I really felt like I was there for his agenda with the students, when a decision this big should be somewhat about me, right? And the reviews said that after surgery, it was impossible to get in touch with him or get a response if you felt like you needed him. The postoperative follow-up was seriously lacking.

Then my miracle came. A heart surgeon friend from another state recommended an orthopedic surgeon who was heralded in the knee specialty world and had actually trained many knee surgeons all over the country. He had designed several of the artificial knees used today and even did research with the PGA Tour. (As a golfer, that really captured me.) I was impressed with his résumé, but I still felt dismayed over my previous experiences and wanted to talk to him. My friend sent me his phone number, and I requested a call with him.

I was surprised to hear from him quickly. He asked me to email my radiology reports, and I did. He called me again and asked about my clinical symptoms over the phone since he lived across the country from me. He wanted to understand my pain picture and know how the knee felt, he said. After asking me some questions, he said that based on the pictures and my descriptions, he thought the other surgeons were right. I needed a new knee. "Straightforward," he said to me.

At this point, the trust window opened for a specific reason. This doctor was obviously competent and understood what was going on. But instead of talking schedule and asking about my insurance, or telling me about how important he was, he began asking about *me*— my life, my need for mobility. He even wanted to know how the knee was affecting my family. He also wanted to know about golf, hobbies, work, activities, and other things important to me. Then, with a great deal of empathy, he began to talk about how this must be terrible for me, how he really wanted to see me on the golf course again and have a full, mobile life. He spoke encouragingly about what my life could be like and said that if I did decide to come to him, they could provide physical therapy for a few weeks and help me reach the point where I could travel home. He even sent me a video of Terry Bradshaw talking about his experience of flying there to have this doc do his knee replacement and how his life was now full again.

This doctor's care for me was the difference between his "genius" and the others'. He seemed to have a different motive. I could sense his love for the work and his intention to move knee replacement science to a different level, but beyond that, he really was interested in moving *me* to a different level. He sounded as motivated to get me back on a golf course as anything else, about being able to take hikes again with my family. He cared about my life. His motive, his intent, was to *help* me.

With that, I decided to fly all the way across the country, with no support system or family other than my one friend and his wife, who took wonderful care of me. The surgeon exceeded my expectations, not only with a successful surgery, but with follow-up and patient care. There was no doubt that he was the real deal, and thankfully, my trust was well-placed.

The lesson I'd like you to take from this story brings us to the second essential of trust: motive, or intent.

In It for the Good of Others

We saw how important being and feeling understood was in the first trust essential, understanding. I would never want a surgeon who did not understand what I needed. But, even when someone understands what you need, it is possible for them to be in it just for themselves and not for you. *Thus, real trust is built not only through understanding but making sure the other party's motive is right, meaning that they are for your good.* I knew the surgeon across the country cared about me. He wanted the best for me. I was more than another paycheck, research project, or professional credit. He truly wanted me to have a better life. He was for my personal good and well-being, and I could tell that it made him happy to know that someone's life was better. That in itself was his reward.

Motive, or intent, is described in many ways, such as:

- "He's in it for the right reasons."
- "Her motives are pure."
- "She cares about me."
- "He cares about me more than he cares about himself."
- "He never thinks about himself. He thinks of others."
- "With her, it's always about the mission or the cause."
- "She would do anything for the kids."
- "He never thinks about his career or position. He thinks about the company and the employees first."
- And many others.

Real trust is built not only through understanding but making sure the other party's motive is right, meaning that they are for your good.

All About "Why"

After I spoke to a university gathering one evening, some students approached me with questions, or just to say "hello." The first one said, "I enjoyed tonight. I'd like to do what you do."

"Great," I said. "Tell me about yourself."

He proceeded to tell me about how he wanted to go to medical school, become a psychiatrist, write books, speak, and be in media. I asked him, "Why?"

He proceeded to list the accomplishments and accolades of his father and grandfather in their careers as prominent physicians, the kind hospitals are named for. He spoke of their standing in their communities and in the medical profession. He said he wanted to follow in their footsteps and be like them. I thought I was going to throw up. Everything he said was motivated by ego and having some sort of standing or image of himself.

His desire had nothing to do with other people. It was all about himself and his pursuit of gaining what he saw as status in his community. I remember thinking, *I hope I know where you practice so I can avoid sending anyone I care about to you.* It was kind of gross.

Then, a second young man came up and mentioned that he enjoyed my talk because he wanted to "do what you do." I asked, "And what is that?"

"I would like to go to medical school, become a psychiatrist, and work in the field and write about these kinds of things as well," he said.

Here we go again, I thought.

"Great. Tell me more," I said, bracing for another narcissistic shower.

"Well, I grew up in the church and have worked with kids since I was in junior high school. I volunteered. I loved it and always thought I wanted to be a youth minister. I just loved working with kids. But in high school, I took biology and fell in love with science. I took every science course I could and started thinking I wanted to go to medical school and become a doctor. But that took me away from the hands-on ministry of helping people deal with their lives and problems and all that I loved. I was really torn. Then, I realized that in psychiatry, I would be able to do both! I could be involved in real-life problems, just as in ministry, and also be in scientific medicine. It was perfect! I could do what I loved and also really serve young people. So that's where I am headed," he replied.

I was stunned. I wanted to scream, "If you can't afford school, call me! I will pay for it!" He was *so* different from the first guy. This one wanted to pursue what he actually loved, and it was just as much about serving and helping *others* as fulfilling his own dream. His *intent, or motive, was to help people.* It was pure, unlike the first one, and it made me instantly trust him.

The second essential of trust—motive—is the one that keeps our entire system wondering about people. "Why is he or she doing this? Who is it really *for*? What are they trying to get out of this? Do they want something good for me too?" These are important questions that everything about us continually wants to decode in order for us to be truly "careless."

When we feel an employer, boss, spouse, friend, church, or institution really does have our best interests at heart, we let down our guard. We rest. We are less apt to guard our wallet, or our heart. We feel some ability to enter into "carelessness." When someone is motivated to have my best interests at heart, I don't worry.

Renowned marriage researcher John Gottman has something he calls the "index of betrayal." It is a metric for knowing when a marriage is in trouble, and it has to do with how much one partner looks out *for* the other. In his words, the marriage is in the trust betrayal zone when "people are no longer looking out for their partner's interests, or looking out for their own interests, but for their own *instead of* their partner's interest. Trust has not only suddenly evaporated but also been replaced by betrayal. One's ally and friend has turned into one's adversary."* The concept here is that in a trusting

---

* John M. Gottman, *The Science of Trust: Emotional Attunement for Couples* (New York: W. W. Norton & Company, 2011), 55. Kindle edition.

relationship, we can depend on the other person to be caring and to look out for us, even when we are not there or not able to.

In another place, he writes: "We can trust that our partner will act in a way that demonstrates caring about how we fare—that is, that our partner is working for our best interests. Our partner 'has our back,' or acts like he or she cares a great deal about our outcomes, our payoffs. Mutual trust would make these gains symmetric. We could say that our partner is 'there for us,' and we are 'there for' our partner."

**Real trust transcends "moral codes," or "duty codes,"
in a powerful way.**

In marriage, think how many problems would be avoided if each partner always asked, "If I do this, what will it feel like to her [or him]?" Or, "How will it affect him [or her or the family]?" There would be no affairs, over-budget spending, pursuits of one's own hobbies, careers, or activities that cause people to abandon their spouses—and no addictions. When a ten-year-old says, "Dad, you always promised to be at my game and you never came. And when I would come home, you would be passed out on the couch," it can finally break through the self-centeredness that allows the addiction to flourish.

In work teams, what if every team member asked, "How is my quality [or timing or emphasis] of work going to affect someone else on the team?" In interdependent work situations, where there is a shared goal with multiple roles, this "thinking of others" is key to making it all work. A little laziness or omissions here and there might not affect me that much, but they could be a real nightmare for someone else. Trust says that your intent is for me as much as it is for yourself.

Real trust transcends "moral codes," or "duty codes," in a powerful way: Love. Care. Compassion. We all grow up learning moral codes such as, "You should share with your sister or friend. That's the right thing to do." But, at some point, we all break a few rules. Rules are not powerful enough. But love is. The addict knows he should not drink so much, but he does. Yet, when he realizes the pain his drinking causes his ten-year-old, his love is a more powerful restrainer than the "rule" of staying sober. Meaningful moral codes depend upon the "law of love." The law of empathy, as we saw, makes us understand someone, and the intent to do them good instead of harm puts that into actionable trust.

Jesus said that all the rules in the entire Bible can be summed up in the law of love: "'Love the Lord your God with all your heart and with all your soul and with all your mind.' This is the first and greatest commandment. And the second is like it: 'Love your neighbor as yourself.' All the Law and the Prophets hang on these two commandments'" (Matt. 22:37-40 NIV).

True love has the motive and intent of first doing no harm, but more than that, looking out for the good of the other person or party. It is about being "for" them as well as "for" ourselves. That way, they can know that we "have their back," so carelessness can begin and guardedness diminish.

Being Motivated "for" Others Can Increase Profits

A major homebuilder I worked with, who has won all sorts of awards, such as Builder of the Year in the US, is a great illustration of what happens when trust is driven by being "for" the other. When founding the company, he valued profitability over size. Being the most profitable builder was a better goal than merely being known as the "biggest." An analytical approach to the dynamics that drive profits made him quickly aware of a common practice at that time in homebuilding: the tendency for builders to work with subcontractors in silos instead of building a community of trust between them. He saw how this disconnected approach significantly affected the bottom line.

In the building business, time is everything. The longer a project takes, the carrying costs of land alone, from the time it's purchased until a development is sold out, can be huge. Anything that reduces that timeline is "found money." So, the builder had an idea. What if one subcontractor began to care for the others' interests in the same way they cared for their part of the project? What if, before they went in to pour concrete in a driveway, they worked with the drywallers to see how a wet driveway would affect the drywallers' ability to move materials into the house? What if they began to take each other's schedules and costs into consideration before simply doing what was good for them? With these questions in mind, in the beginning of his projects, the builder started meeting with everyone involved to ask: "What's good for you? We want to understand that and do our work in a way that helps you work more efficiently." Not waiting in line helps everyone, as each subcontractor has its own schedules and needs to move quickly as well.

True love has the motive and intent of first doing no harm, but more than that, looking out for the good of the other person or party.

The results were exponential. As they began to care for each other's timelines and extra inconveniences, everyone profited. The builder was able to complete projects much more quickly, as were the subcontractors. And profit margins got much better.

This approach may seem like common sense, but at that time, the building industry was dominated by "gunslinger" independent types who worked to drive their own interests and get things done, not thinking much about how their piece of the project affected everyone else.

The builder's new approach to subcontractors inspired great loyalty to him and his company, which brought even more preferred treatment in pricing and go-aheads for projects. In short, the subcontractors trusted him because he created an environment in which they felt others were looking out for them. It was not just about the builder, so timelines got shorter, and costs went down.

When the motive is to benefit others and not just ourselves, everyone profits.

What if every company, inside and out, before doing their work, asked: "How will this affect the others involved?" When the motive is to benefit others and not just ourselves, everyone profits.

Maximizing Trust in a Higher Motive

In the mid-1990s, a small group of regulators from the federal government, some executives from the airline industry, and pilot union leaders came together to attack the problem of airline crashes. There were simply too many. The regulators decided that there needed to be a coming together of everyone in a high atmosphere of trust to disclose, voluntarily, safety incidents with each other so they could all work on the problems together. It was going to require information sharing, with no fear of punishment for airlines or pilots when mistakes were shared. The stakes were high, and there were many doubters in the beginning of the program—for fear of being exposed, disciplined, sued, or careers ended if one's mistakes were made known.

Nevertheless, the emphasis on trust was pushed forward, and carelessness was allowed to rule.

As airline safety writer Andy Pasztor says, "Their approach was simple in its fundamentals but wickedly difficult to implement at the start, requiring unprecedented levels of trust among the participants. During the early stages, representatives of pilots and carriers grudgingly agreed to share information with each other, as well as with the government, regarding budding hazards and near-crashes. Tentative cooperation was dependent on FAA pledges that good-faith mistakes and procedural violations wouldn't result in enforcement actions." Said another way, this was big-time scary and required more trust than was imaginable to make happen.

But the trust was kept. And the results were unprecedented. As Pasztor reports, "In 1996 US carriers had a fatal accident rate of roughly one crash for every two million departures. That year alone, more than 350 people died in domestic airline accidents, including 230 in the infamous fuel-tank explosion on TWA Flight 800 that sucked scores of passengers out of the fractured fuselage. Within 10 years, the fatal accident rate had been reduced by more than 80%, beating a goal set by a White House commission." Pasztor goes on to report that this figure went on to be reduced to one for every 120 million departures. Said another way, "Over the past 12 years, U.S. airlines have accomplished an astonishing feat: carrying more than eight billion passengers without a fatal crash."[*]

It is amazing to see the power of trust operating in this incredible accomplishment. Without trust, none of this could have happened. And the dynamic that drove that trust was exactly what we are referring to here: the putting aside of one's own interests in the service

---

[*] "The Airline Safety Revolution: The Airline Industry's Long Path to Safer Skies," *Wall Street Journal* (April 17, 2021).

of others. In this instance, that service was to a higher purpose: the safety of the passengers.

One of the most powerful drivers of trust is knowing that someone's motive is rooted in a higher calling principle or value that transcends their own interests. I recently conducted a retreat for the executive team of a major US company. Their accomplishments had been remarkable, outpacing their competitors exponentially and returning massive equity growth for their stockholders. The team had just emerged from successfully managing the worst of COVID, and it was time to set the next season's strategy.

To begin the retreat, I wanted to see how the team of executives grasped the strengths that had driven their success in the previous couple of years and how well they understood what had happened and why. I gave them a simple assignment to begin: "Take a few minutes and write down what you think is the greatest strength of this team."

When they turned in their answers, I was astonished. I have never seen such unity among a group of executives. Unanimously, they said their greatest strength was one thing: "our commitment to our corporate purpose." Not one person said it was their marketing savvy, their innovation, their creativity, or their research and development. They all said their greatest strength was their unity around the corporate purpose. And here's the real magic: their corporate purpose is centered around serving others.

The fact that they all served a higher purpose allowed them to behave and to execute in a manner that everyone could trust. There was no silo behavior, no pushing of departmental agendas, no careerism to be found. They were all devoted to the higher purpose they had come together to achieve.

This resulted in an unprecedented level of collaboration—sharing resources, people, information, power, and the like. These people truly worked together. Certainly, they had different opinions at times, but in a way that was always in search of "the best answer" instead of "my best interests." These were not people who didn't care about profits or accomplishments; they did. But they weren't only motivated by profits. Their driving force was serving others and the purpose of the company.

As a result, the employees of this company trusted each other. When someone did something another person might question, the question wasn't rooted in suspicion. Instead, it came from an attitude of "I wonder why she did that? I know she must have had a good reason." This kind of trust goes a long way to avoid politics and division.

Trust is a powerful force, and as we've seen, it yields powerful results in everything from brain development to marriage to economics. The takeaway here is that trust increases when we know that someone's motive is not just about themselves but about us or about a higher purpose that we value as well.

Now, let's look at trust element number three.

SIX

ABILITY:
THE THIRD ESSENTIAL OF TRUST

Let's return to my search for a knee surgeon. As you remember, my trust grew when I felt my doctor fulfilled the first two essentials of trust: he understood me, and his motive was "for" me. Put yourself in my shoes for a moment. You've just found a doctor who really gets you and really cares for you. You're ready to move forward with the knee replacement, right? Sure—unless the conversation continues like this:

"Let's get you scheduled for this surgery. I want to make sure you don't have to wait for months. The calendar fills up pretty fast," he says. Now you're feeling even better about his concern for you and how he looks out for you; your trust is high and growing.

"And," he continues as you walk to the scheduling desk, "I am so excited to operate on your knee. It is an amazing procedure and I have always wanted to do one. I'm an ob-gyn. I never get a chance to do knees, and this is really going to be fun for me. I need a change of pace, and I'm really looking forward to it."

Ooops. Dr. He-Understands-and-Cares-for-Me just lost your trust. I hope you'd be running for the door at this point. For sure, understanding and motive are essential to trust. Essential. But as we are seeing, trust involves several factors, and the one we'll explore in this chapter is crucial: the third essential of trust is ability, or capacity. This means a person can deliver what you are trusting him or her to deliver. It's being able to do what you need them to do.

Dr. Understanding-and-Care may be a great ob-gyn, but that does not equip him to have the abilities needed to carve on my knee. In my search for a knee surgeon, ability was extremely important to me. I was looking for someone capable of delivering what I trusted him to deliver: a good new knee, not a new baby.

Understanding and motive must be supported by ability.

As I shared in chapter 5, the doctor I ultimately chose to perform my operation was very understanding and his intent was to care for me. His motive was clearly good. But I needed more. I had to ask, "How good is he?"

As I investigated his abilities, I found some serious qualifications. He had recently been elected president of the American Association of Hip and Knee Surgeons, has lectured extensively around the world, and trained many surgeons at some of the finest hospitals around the country, including in Los Angeles, where I live. In addition, he held several patents for the artificial knee joints that are placed in people's legs. He actually invented them. Then, as I alluded to in the previous chapter, I discovered that he conducts research on golfers and knees with the PGA Tour. On top of all this, he does nearly 1,000 knee replacements a year, which should leave someone with adequate practice. He has already had his mulligans. Long story short: *I found my guy*. I have some good friends who are ob-gyns, but I felt good that he was going to be my surgeon instead of them. Everything I learned about him increased my trust in his ability to do what I would entrust to him to do.

As we look at a model of trust, the point here is this: understanding and motive must be supported by ability. Someone can be a wonderful and capable person in many ways but not be someone we want to trust in a *specific* way.

It Happens All the Time

The founder and chairman of the board of a company reached out to me, saying, "I need some help, a coach for our CEO. Can we get together and talk?" I agreed and we set a time to meet.

Unfortunately, the story he relayed was a familiar one. Like Colin and Shannon, this founder was dealing with a disappointing new CEO. But unlike Colin's and Shannon's hire, this one actually had great understanding, motive, and other qualities of trust. Yet, one important one was missing: the *ability* needed in the context of a specific role.

He told me that their new CEO, in the position for a year and a half, seemed to be floundering. He observed that the company felt stagnated in some way, like the energy had drained out of it and it didn't seem to be "moving." It was just going through the motions, but not particularly feeling proactive and driving toward a future. In addition, he said, some internal surveys showed that morale and engagement were down.

As I delved into the situation and interviewed the executive team and others, I learned some important things. First, everyone really loved the new CEO, Bradley. He was a wonderful person— caring, smart, and accomplished. He had served as the company's COO for several years before taking this job. He had always gotten great reviews and his performance had been stellar. He had led many initiatives that had streamlined operations, fixed supply chain issues, revamped research and development, and accomplished other important objectives. Impressive.

But, since he had become CEO, there were some new trends. First of all, people felt as though the energy in the company had waned over time. They used words such as *listless* and *anemic*. They sensed an absence of forward motion. Also, several members of the executive team felt a bit micromanaged in their reporting relationship with Bradley. They felt he was "too much in the weeds." But overwhelmingly they felt a loss of direction and simply being busy. *"Where are we headed?"* was a common question among them.

What was becoming clear to me was that they didn't have a CEO. They still had a COO. But he had the position of CEO. "How did this happen?" I wondered. So, I asked the board chairman.

"Bradley has been with us for a long time. He understood the company better than anyone at his level. And his performance was incredible. He re-engineered so much, and I always thought about him as the guy who 'helped us be better.' He improved everything he touched. So, when our former CEO was ready to retire, Bradley seemed like the biggest star we had, and we promoted him to CEO," he explained.

"So, where did he get the 'E'?" I asked.

"What?" he asked.

"He was COO, and you made him CEO. Where did he get the 'E'?" I asked again.

"We promoted him to CEO. That's how it happened," he reiterated.

"I know he got the CEO *job*. But a CEO position needs vastly different capabilities than the COO job. The abilities that a CEO must possess do overlap with those of a COO in some ways, but they are distinct. They include an 'E,' not just an 'O.'"

He asked me to continue, and we talked at length about the difference in the two positions. Bradley was stellar at "operations." He made everything operate and operate better than it did. He improved what was already there. He made it all work, which was great—for a COO.

But a CEO has something called "executive functions of an organization," which begin with being able to define a state that doesn't yet exist, to see the future, if you will. We call this *vision*. A CEO is responsible for seeing the future and leading the organization into that future by engaging the appropriate talent and building the right culture, setting a strategy, and steering the ship toward that future reality. The CEO also has to build external alliances in the context of the business and make sure the energy and resources needed will be available— relationships, financing, seeing and negotiating obstacles to the vision and strategy, and on and on. The CEO needs to be able to see where things need to go and to make sure the organization gets there. An operations executive makes sure those components operate well and that things get done. But the burden of the future usually rests primarily on the CEO and that person generates much of the energy to move toward it.

Bradley was acting like an operator, not like a CEO, and the company felt it. People perceived the lack of future orientation, innovation, and energy. They didn't feel engaged around a big enough vision to keep them feeling purposeful and excited. They just felt they were "doing their jobs," and Bradley was mostly focused on making sure they were.

The board had a choice to make. One option was to get Bradley some "E"—the abilities that he did not have but could develop with the right coaching, modeling, and training. Their other option was to get some "E" by finding someone else for the CEO position. Neither was necessarily right or wrong, but much wisdom was required to make the decision. (I won't tell you what they did, lest you think it would be the right one in all circumstances.)

My point in sharing this story is that the board had entrusted the company to someone who *did not have the ability to deliver what they entrusted him to deliver—the "E" ability.*

Remember, people had felt Bradley had understood them for years. They believed his "motives" were pure and that he cared about the company, its mission, and its people. He had the first two essentials of trust. But the third one was lacking: ability.

This does happen all the time. People make big trust decisions because they already trust someone in many ways. The person is caring, honest, works hard, has good values, and is understanding and pure-hearted, smart, and creative. He or she probably has many other positive traits too. So, the "trust" button gets pushed, and they entrust something to such a good person. Usually, they really like the person, are already close friends, or have had great experiences with them, and these dynamics also make them trust the person. *But this is a mistake because the person doesn't have the ability needed to be trusted— not in the specific way or context in which they are about to be trusted.*

Think about the following situation. Someone falls "in love" with a great, honest, fun person. After a period of dating bliss, they hit the "trust button" and enter into marriage. But marriage takes more than love, honesty, and fun. There are some very important "abilities" required to make it work. Does this person have the ability to communicate, to resolve conflict, to be resilient under stress, to be a good mother or father to your future children, and to be financially responsible? How many marriages have you seen struggle or fail because these "abilities" were absent? Yet people frequently entrust their entire lives to people who don't have the ability to be a good spouse, wrongly thinking they will be able to deliver on the marriage contract.

Consider this scenario. Two friends have so much fun together. They have the same values, and both are hard-working at their jobs. Yet, when they sit around and muse about their futures, they'd like all the fun they have as friends to carry over into their work. They wish they could work together so they could enjoy all of life like they enjoy their friendship. So they go into business together. After a while, one of them realizes that someone may have the abilities necessary to be a great friend and not have the abilities to run their own business.

That person is much better suited for a job than for being a business owner. The partner finds himself or herself unequally yoked to a friend they can't trust to do their part in the business. He or she is not a bad person, just a bad choice as a business partner. (I actually had one case like this in which after several years, one of the partners offered to pay the other best friend-partner a million dollars a year to *not be involved in the business anymore*.)

A family has a small business. There are three grown kids, but only one of them has an interest in going into the business. Yet, they all are stakeholders, meaning their financial future is in some way tied up in the family business. The parents really would like the business to stay in the family, and Joey wants to take it over. And he is the only one who wants to do it. So he is given the reins. Why? *Because he is family.* We *trust him.* He is a good person and he wants it. But, soon, things do not go well. Joey, while being a "good person," is not capable of running the business. Employees leave, revenues go down, etc. And now, the siblings are really upset. They are not getting the profit-sharing checks that they had planned on for sending their kids to school, being able to buy a home, and other benefits they had for just being fortunate enough to be in this family while their parents were in charge of the company. Mom and Dad had entrusted the family's future to a great son, but who did not have the ability needed to run the business. Maybe, as discussed above, he could have acquired that ability *if they had required him to grow into the role through working somewhere else, succeeding, and then climbing the ranks in their business while he developed the abilities needed.* But, they didn't think of ability primarily; they thought of *relationship.* Ability was needed for that kind of trust. A good relationship is never enough for a specific ability.

Let me ask you to think about one more situation because it is so common in certain circles. A homeowner needs a contractor for a remodel and meets one at church. They are so happy to have found someone they can trust—because they found that person at church.

They say, "Contractors are difficult to trust, but this one is a fellow Christian, so we feel really good about him. So thankful!" But, as nice as he seemed, they should have looked a little deeper below the surface. Or maybe they should have read their Bible, since it teaches that all sorts of people call themselves Christians—some trustworthy and good, some horrible and outright criminal. But because of an immediate "connection" and the notion that a Christian should be honest and competent, they go forward. After delays, price overruns, and an uneven floor, they later wish they had vetted his abilities a little more thoroughly.

We could list more, but you have seen it and probably done it as well, as we all have. For many reasons that are good, such as the ones in the scenarios I've described, we extend trust to someone to deliver what we entrust to them, yet we do not look closely enough at the specific ability that is necessary for them to come through in the ways that we need them.

Note to self: You can really like someone, and trust them in many ways, yet not be able to trust them in *specific* ways that are important. And it is okay to say no and not move forward in that arena.

It's Okay to Ask for Proof

A friend told me his daughter's boyfriend had invited him to have dinner and he thought the young man was going to ask for his daughter's hand in marriage. He asked me, "What do I ask him? How does this work?"

"I know what I'll do when I get that call," I said.

"What?" he asked.

"I will say, 'Great. I'll look forward to it.' Then, if he does ask for her hand, I will say, 'Let's get together again. Bring your tax returns from the past two years and your credit report. We can talk some more then,'" I said.

My friend laughed and said, "Right. But seriously. What will you say?"

"I told you. I am serious," I replied.

"That's crazy," he said. "I don't want him to think I'm interested in how much money he has. That's kind of rude," he said.

"I don't care about the money," I said. "Tell him to white out the numbers if he wants. What I want to know is, does he even have the tax returns and the credit report? Does he have the ability to manage his life in such a competent way that he can even *find* his tax returns and a document showing how he has managed his commitments to lenders? If he can't be trusted to manage his own life, how can my daughter trust him to manage their life together? I'm looking for *trustworthiness*, not big balances or income," I said.

My friend and I had a good discussion. I'm not sure if he went through with the meeting with his daughter's boyfriend in the way that I plan to, but it gave him a whole new way to think about the conversation. It helped him move past, "Is the young man a good person?" Now he was asking, "Is this man ready to take on the responsibilities of marriage and can he show me that he has the capacity to make it successful?"

Often, when people enter into arenas of trust with people they know or like, a kind of halo effect goes to work toward that person and they trust them in unvetted arenas. I'll say it again: the fact that someone is a good person does not mean you can trust them to perform in all arenas. One of the situations in which I have seen this happen over and over again is on church or nonprofit boards. Someone will get a vision to start a church or a charity and will have several people in their circle who are supportive and "spiritually mature." Sometimes they will have people with the financial wherewithal to help meet their funding needs. Those people will be asked to join the board of the new organization.

The problem arises when the church or the organization grows to a point where it needs a board that has some real depth in specific areas of expertise, *especially board expertise.* Many of these people have never served on a board or do not have deep knowledge in any area that pertains to the work. They were chosen simply because they were supportive, wealthy, influential, spiritual, or a good friend. These are hardly qualifications for board abilities.

Then, the organization finds itself in a tough season—financially, legally, or in some other way—and the founding leader has to turn to outsiders for guidance because the people on the board don't have the abilities the organization needs from its board; the board is weak. At that point, there is a crisis to figure out how to change the board, to form another board to operate with a different title in a parallel way, or some other work-around. Had adequate trust work been done in the beginning, this would not happen. Nor would we have as many "yes" boards as we do. Often, friends will just say "yes" to anything the founder wants, to the detriment of the organization and its stakeholders.

No leader should feel the isolation of not having a strong board to turn to, and every leader needs a board capable of ensuring that he or she is accountable and served well by the board. But without proper vetting of abilities that will be needed later, this scenario sadly happens frequently.

Similarly, how I wish that families would vet and train their grown children to have the ability to handle an inheritance, even a small one. Many problems could be averted. I once heard someone give a powerful response when asked how he thought about passing on an inheritance. The amount of the inheritance doesn't matter; the same principles apply. He said, "All I have is not mine anyway. It belongs to God. I am just a steward for my lifetime. And part of my being a good steward is to pick the next steward or stewards well. So, my kids have been told that they will be evaluated as to how they use money as I get older, and I will pass it on to the next steward or stewards, the one or ones who show themselves to have good ability to use money well."

Wow. I wanted to cheer for this man and his wisdom.

This is exactly the model Jesus speaks of in the parable of the talents (Matt. 25:14-29). The steward who did well with what he was given was given more, and the one who did not perform well lost his opportunity. His talents were then given to the one who had proven himself capable of managing them successfully. He could trust that steward.

Suitable to Trust

The history of the word *ability* teaches us that it comes from the meaning around being "suitable."* This is a perfect way to think about this element of trust. Is it suitable for you to trust this particular aspect of life to this person? Is this person suitable for the task? Can he or she deliver what you need?

Some people may wonder if this concept sounds like perfectionism or judgment—as though I'm encouraging people to be too harsh to evaluate others. But many marriages, businesses, friendships, family relationships, and the like would disagree—after the fact. They wish that they had done a little more evaluation to figure out whether someone was suitable for the trust they had been given.

This is in no way arrogant. In fact, when we apply it to ourselves, it leads us to humility. Which of us would say that we are suitable to be trusted with a friend's brain surgery? Not many. Even if we are friends. This doesn't mean you and I are not "okay" or trustworthy in other ways. It simply means that in some specific areas of trust, we don't qualify. If I were you, I would not trust me to fix your car or

---

* Douglas Harper, "Etymology of ability," Online Etymology Dictionary, updated October 31, 2021, https://www.etymonline.com/word/ability.

build you a house. I'm absolutely not suitable for your trust in those arenas. Hopefully you could trust me to give some kinds of psychological assistance in the process, but nothing mechanical for sure. This principle applies to the way you evaluate others as well. Do not feel queasy about questioning whether or not someone might be able to deliver what you need done, and possibly saying "no" when the answer is no. That is wisdom and it is okay.

Withholding trust on the basis of ability is not cut-and-dried. Someone may grow into being trustworthy in an area in which they currently aren't. That could have happened with Bradley. The answer is sometimes, "Not right now, but possibly later." There are many good people in whom we would want to entrust something and simply aren't ready at this time, but can be made ready with the right training and experiences. Ability can grow, so don't burn your bridges or tell everyone that they are disqualified for life just because they don't have the capacity for something specific today. People grow, and they may have the ability you need tomorrow. That "wannabe fiancé" asking for your daughter's hand could grow suitable with the right steps.

Now you know three essentials of trust: understanding, motive, and ability. Let's see what number four looks like.

CHARACTER:
THE FOURTH ESSENTIAL OF TRUST

Put yourself in my place again regarding a knee replacement. You've chosen a surgeon who understands you deeply and you feel his empathy. You know he is "for" you and wants the best for you. He is deeply motivated for you to regain your ability to function and live a fulfilling life. And, certainly he has proven to be skilled and capable. Then, in an unusual move, he invites you to join the audience in the operating theater so you can see how this surgery is done. (Admittedly, theater observation isn't usually extended to an actual patient of their own doctor, but go with me here.) *That sounds great*, you think. *Then I'll really know what my surgery will entail.* "Let's do it," you say.

The procedure begins, and everything seems to be going smoothly. Then it happens. Suddenly, the patient begins to bleed profusely, in a way you know is unexpected. You see the team moving into different positions and responding, grabbing this instrument and that one. But something that shocks you happens next. Your surgeon screams, "He's bleeding! What did you idiots do? Somebody do something! Stop this bleeding or you'll be next!" And from there continues to yell at people and seems to cause more chaos than he relieves. You can tell the surgical team is clearly rattled at his outbursts. They are trying to work and deal with getting screamed at all at the same time.

85

And you—your trust in "Dr. Understanding-Good Motive-Capable-Trustworthy" has turned to despair. It wasn't because of a lack of skill, but because of something else altogether: his character, his personal makeup, how he's wired. You've witnessed a lack of what business and leadership people call "soft skills"—the collection of personal traits someone possesses that dictate how he or she approaches people, relationships, tasks, stress, difficulties, conflict, fear, goals, emotions, and the like. In the last few decades, some of this has been referred to as "emotional intelligence." It is about personal makeup and how people deal with others, themselves, and life. And as you got a glimpse of your surgeon's poor soft skills when you saw how he acts under pressure, your trust disappears.

Elevating Our View of Character

Often, when we speak of "character," especially when wondering, "Can you trust him?" we say things like, "Oh, I totally trust him." We mean that this is a person who would not lie, cheat, or steal. In other words, *we tend to see the person only through a moral or ethical lens.* We think that if someone has good character, it simply means we can believe the numbers. It's like the way people often use the word *integrity*. A person of integrity is often described basically as someone who can be trusted to be honest. Again, he or she does not lie, cheat, or steal. So many assume the person is trustworthy.

This is far from the truth of the deeper and *necessary* meanings of *integrity* and *character*, as well as the meaning of *trustworthy*. There are many people who would not lie, cheat, or steal, but we would be in error to trust them in many arenas of life because of the rest of their personal makeup. You've probably had bosses, friends, or even family members who would not lie, cheat, or steal—but given another chance to work with them closely, you would certainly pass. You don't want to deal with them again. Why? Because they have other "issues" that get in the way of things going well, and you are not able to trust them when you need things to work out well or even to be drama-free. Those people may be smart, honest, and "capable," but so difficult to work with or falling short in other ways that it just won't work.

Both the Bible and psychological research speak of the necessity of having personal traits that are *more than the moral qualities of honesty and ethical behavior in order to be depended upon, to be trusted to deliver results*. The apostle Peter puts it like this:

> *For this very reason, make every effort to add to your faith virtue; and to virtue, knowledge; and to knowledge, self-control; and to self-control, perseverance; and to perseverance, godliness; and to godliness, brotherly kindness; and to brotherly kindness, love. For if you possess these qualities and continue to grow in them, they will keep you from being ineffective and unproductive in your knowledge of our Lord Jesus Christ. But whoever lacks these traits is nearsighted to the point of blindness, having forgotten that he has been cleansed from his past sins.* —2 Peter 1:5-9 BSB

This passage contains a great list of soft skills, the same ones you see showing up in the leadership literature:

Virtue

Virtue is a quality of someone who seeks goodness and has high moral character—the way we usually think of character. Honesty is certainly bedrock. But virtue is also more than that, as Merriam-Webster says. It includes "a beneficial quality or power of a thing," "courage," "merit," "a capacity to act," and "chastity."*

---

* "Virtue," Merriam-Webster, updated November 6, 2022, https://www.merriam-webster.com/dictionary/virtue.

Knowledge

The Greek word used in this passage for *knowledge* means applied wisdom. A person who has knowledge has the experience to apply themselves and their knowledge well to *real* life.

Self-Control

What good does it do to try to trust someone who is impulsive, or angry, or lacks self-control in an area, no matter how smart they are? If people cannot control themselves, we cannot trust them to act well or wisely. How many marriages, relationships, families, businesses, and ministries have been wrecked because of the absence of self-control? Financially? Emotionally? Sexually?

Perseverance

Usually, the areas in which we need to be able to trust someone are areas where life can get difficult. We often need to depend on someone during problematic times and through various struggles. If someone cannot persevere through struggle or through a difficult task, project, obstacle, or conflict, we cannot trust them to deliver in the end. In marriage, persevering through a tough season is essential to making it long-term. And in business, persevering through tough seasons is essential to long-term success. Sticking it out, keeping going when things are hard, and getting to a good conclusion is everything.

Godliness

Godliness is a term that refers to "someone's inner response to the things of God, which shows itself in reverence."[*] No matter how anyone expresses their spiritual beliefs, we know the real thing when

---

[*] James Strong, *The New Strong's Expanded Exhaustive Concordance of the Bible* (Nashville, TN: Thomas Nelson, 2010).

genuine spirituality shows up instead of empty religiosity. True inner reverence and depth are apparent, and they invite our trust.

Brotherly Kindness

This term means being a "loving friend," or having "affection for brothers or sisters."* How many marriages in conflict, even between "honest" people, have lost the kindness needed to make it work? Or work teams? Or extended families? Or contractual relationships? All of these problem scenarios can happen with an honest person who lacks kindness. In fact, some of the least kind individuals are people of rigid rules and moralistic, judgmental "integrity." But without the demonstration of kindness, trust does not ensue. Oxytocin will *not* show up in the absence of kindness. Ask an infant.

Without the demonstration of kindness, trust does not ensue.

Love

The Greek word used for "love," *agape*, in this passage is deep, but its overall flavor is one of goodwill and benevolence for someone. It is acting toward a person with "preference." How good it feels, how much trust we extend, when someone acts toward us with "preference." We are a VIP to them, in every sense of the term. Oxytocin abounds when we are treated this way.

My point in exploring the character traits in just this one passage of Scripture is to show that character is more than morality. But, don't

---

* Strong, *The New Strong's Expanded Exhaustive Concordance of the Bible.*

get me wrong. For sure, without the foundation of honesty, ethical behavior, and the absence of "lying, cheating, and stealing," we have *nothing*. Let me put it this way:

> Where there is lying, cheating, or stealing, there can be no trust. Zero.

As Proverbs 25:19 says, "Like a broken tooth or a lame foot is reliance on the unfaithful in a time of trouble" (NIV). In fact, 2 Peter 1:5-6 *begins* with the moral foundation: *Virtue*. This refers to high *moral* character, and there is a reason the passage begins with it. We cannot ever forget that honesty and moral integrity are the "permission to play" traits. Without these, we cannot even talk about trust.

Honesty must be addressed first. I have seen more marriages ruined *not* by mistakes or betrayals, but by continuous lying about something they were not revealing. The mistake could have been forgiven, but the ongoing lies—the continual cover-up—killed the trust, not necessarily the affair or the "betrayal." Honesty is crucial and foundational.

I am so intent on helping you to see that character is more than honesty and ethics that I fear not saying this strongly enough, so I will repeat it once more: without basic character traits of honesty, transparency, lack of duplicity (being the same person in public and private), responsibility, high morals, and others, we cannot have trust. So, as we go forward in seeing that a lack of trust can come from *more* than the absence of basic character qualities, let's make sure that we know that a *lack* of honesty and morality cannot be tolerated or trusted, nor can it go unaddressed. It is essential; it's bedrock. If you can't believe a person, you have nothing to stand on.

Again though, to go further, the important point here is that character is more than honesty and ethical behavior. It also includes the personal traits, the makeup of qualities needed in a person for whatever you are trusting them for in that relationship. In many contexts, if those traits are missing, the trust will fail.

The president of a large Christian organization once called me to do some leadership development with his executive team. In our first meeting, I said, "I'm really looking forward to working with you. I've admired the work this organization does for so long. And I love getting to work in a Christian organization because most of my work is in the business world and here we can talk about the spiritual aspects of leadership as well. This'll be fun for me."

I have seen more marriages ruined *not* by mistakes or betrayals, but by continuous lying about something they were not revealing.

When I spoke about "the spiritual aspects of leadership," I thought his hair might catch on fire. He got very animated and said emphatically, "Wait! Hold on. We don't need any spiritual stuff here. These are very godly people—very spiritually mature. What we need is *leadership* development, not anything spiritual."

"Well, I do think they have a lot to do with each other, but tell me, what leadership issues are you finding?"

He talked about how he could not get the team to work together. He said that most of them were protecting their own departments, their own people, and their own agendas, budgets, and the like. He couldn't get them to share information, resources, and sometimes people and funds when it would benefit the shared goal and vision. They stiff-armed each other at times when collaboration would have been much better.

So I asked, "These are the 'godly, spiritually mature' people you were talking about?"

"Yes," he responded. "They are all very spiritually mature."

"Well, with all due respect," I said, "my Bible says that love 'does not seek its own' [1 Cor. 13:5 NASB]. It also says that to be fruitful, leaders need to exhibit 'mutual affection' [2 Peter 1:7 NIV]. In your team, I see a lot of 'seeking their own' and very little mutuality here, for starters. So, whether or not you call this spiritual development or leadership development doesn't matter to me. But we have to get it fixed if this team is going to accomplish the big mission you have laid out for them. And based on what you've said, I wouldn't call them 'godly' or 'mature' either. I think they have some work to do."

The list of character traits from 2 Peter 1:5-9 comes from a spiritual or faith context, the Bible. But secular business research affirms these qualities too. As I said to him, wherever it comes from, whether from faith traditions or secular leadership and psychological research, the issue is always the same: *character matters.* And character includes more than just honesty and morality, which he was confusing with maturity.

To take it out of the faith context, let's consider the field of "emotional intelligence" (EQ), which has become a widespread term to describe a number of personal traits that are essential for success in both personal and professional settings. Generally, the traits involve many of the same ones listed in 2 Peter, and much research has been done that validates how important these personal qualities are to people's success. For example, Harvard Business School research showed that EQ counts for twice as much as people's intelligence and other professional skills in terms of how successful they become.[*]

* Laura Wilcox, "Emotional Intelligence Is No Soft Skill," Professional Development, Harvard Division of Continuing Education, July 6, 2015, https://professional.dce.harvard.edu/blog/emotional-intelligence-is-no-soft-skill.

Broadly, EQ deals with domains such as self-awareness, relation-ship management, self-management, and social awareness. From these come several other personal qualities and abilities that give someone the capacity to work well with themselves and with other people. How do they handle their emotions and the emotions of others? How in control of themselves are they? How adaptable are they when things go awry? Are they positive or negative? Can they work with others well? And more.

While this is not a book on character, personality, or emotional intelligence, it is a book on trust. My point here is that trust is a multi-dimensional construct, as we have said, and one of those dimensions is how a person is constructed—his or her character. What EQ and related research shows is that this dimension is as important as any other in terms of trusting someone in specific ways. It helps us under-stand how a person will perform their technical, professional, or other competencies in a particular context. It teaches us that no matter how gifted or smart or charming they are, we must know what they are like as *people*. We need to understand how they manage themselves, others, and tasks. EQ can lead to great trustworthiness, or disasters, pain, drama, and failure.

We need to be able to trust that someone's makeup and character can deliver on what we have entrusted to them.

Think back to contexts or relationships when someone was full of what we call "integrity," but you were ultimately dissatisfied with the relationship. They were honest, but emotionally unavailable or distant. They had "integrity" but were controlling. Or perfectionistic.

Or hard driving. Or unorganized. Or without empathy or compassion when needed. Arrogant? Narcissistic? Shall I go on?

We need to be able to trust that someone's makeup and character can deliver on what we have entrusted to them. This is very important, regardless of any other good qualities they may have.

In a wonderful book called *The Checklist Manifesto*, the author, Atul Gawande, details a fascinating narrative about the adoption of checklists in several fields, including medicine. One of the areas he discusses is the operating room and the problems that occur because of mistakes made by people who know what to do but sometimes miss something, overlook something, or make some other error unrelated to competency. A simple checklist can avoid many of these mistakes from being made. In fact, in just one of his experiments, here are the results he recorded in eight hospitals when an operating room team had high trust and used a checklist to make sure nothing was missed:

- The rate of complications fell by 36%.
- Deaths fell by 47%.
- Infections fell by almost half.
- Expected serious complications in difficult cases fell from 435 to 277, sparing 150 from harm and 27 from death.
- Patients needing to return to the operating room after the original operation because of bleeding or other problems fell by one-fourth.

Throughout the book, Gawande gives more evidence of the power of a checklist to overcome human error. But there was also a difficult dynamic that rendered checklists completely ineffectual: the resistance of some surgeons to implementing the checklist.

Some surgeons were annoyed by it, seeing it as a waste of time. Some surgeons could not relinquish the authoritarian control culture so common in hospitals that make others in the OR fearful to speak up if they see an error. There is a longstanding tradition in the culture of medicine that believes that what is needed is a kind of "expert audacity," and checklists seem too elementary to arrogant surgeons. With that kind of "audacity" attitude by a surgeon, nurses or others in the OR have a fear of getting rebuffed by an angry surgeon with a senior position. So, they are afraid to speak up or participate. Or a surgeon thinks that it is "below my expertise" to have these people "check on me." Wow. Attitude matters.

So in spite of extremely high stakes and sound research, character issues such as arrogance, control, anger, and impatience were still getting in the way of building the kind of trust in the OR where good results could occur and bad ones be avoided. Trust fueled life-saving results, but that trust could only exist where the personalities involved could build it. This is a great example of where "character matters." Surgeons can understand the patient, want the best for them, have the needed expertise, but still have a character issue that prevents an operating room from functioning at its best possible level. This keeps them for doing what is best for their patients, and that renders them really, really unworthy of trust. Character matters.

Character Has Specificity

When my sister-in-law got engaged, she and her fiancé, Mark, asked me to perform their wedding. I am not a pastor, but I was really moved that they would want me to do the ceremony and help them tie the knot. So, I got ordained for a day by a local church (that's about as long as they could trust me to be "holy"), and we decided to go forward.

Since I knew her and Mark well, I thought for the premarital counseling they should have someone more objective. I asked them to see a local pastor to go through the normal premarital counseling process. The pastor agreed and began by giving them a battery of tests, including one test that measures sympathy, including how well they communicated empathy to people. When we got together for their first session, the pastor said to them, "I am a little worried about you guys."

"Why?" they asked.

"Because you both got the lowest score possible on the sympathy scale," he said. "Who is going to be the caring one in this relationship?"

After the initial shock, we all started laughing and began to discuss the different ways in which their love was expressed. And their relationship was great. But, the test was accurate about a certain kind of trait. They were both pretty tough-skinned people. Very, very loving and giving, but not exactly "soft." Mark, for example, was a Navy SEAL, and softness was just not part of his profile. Love and sacrifice, yes. Softness, no.

So what does this mean? It means that Mark would not be my first choice to entrust with a very sensitive, emotionally fragile person. He might look at them and say something I heard one of his SEAL buddies say one time: "We are all about doing what is needed to be done to complete the mission. We might get wounded or injured, but we always remember and tell ourselves, 'Pain is temporary. So ignore it and focus.' Press on, be strong, no paying attention to minor inconveniences that might derail you, such as bone-searing pain."

That's great for a shootout behind enemy lines in some foreign country where you have to survive to get back to safety, but it is not a helpful trait for someone needing sensitive emotional care.

Who would I entrust a patient like that to? Someone with a lot of compassion, empathy, understanding, and some serious emotional awareness of others.

But if I found myself under attack or in danger, I would be calling for Mark in a heartbeat, not the softhearted psych nurse. He would rush in and take them down. I would trust him with my life in that scenario. Let me make this point another way: a person's trustworthiness is specific to the certain areas in which we trust them. Keeping this in mind will help keep us from being too perfectionistic about trust. We don't need someone to be perfect in every area of their makeup. We all have strengths, weaknesses, and deficiencies. We can accept and value a person in the midst of what they do not do well. The important question is *can they do what we need them to do for that context?* This is where trust either gets built, or dinged.

When we realize this, we can love and appreciate someone for their strengths and in spite of their weaknesses or deficiencies. In a marriage where the couple values each other for their differences, you will hear each partner laughing at what the other one does not possess. "Are you kidding? Send him to pick up all of the ingredients we need for the party?" the wife may say, "No way. He is too scattered and forgetful, and he would come home with only half of what's on the list. I need him to be here and greet guests because he makes every-one feel included and happy to be here. But I can't trust him to get the list right. I'll do that." And then they both laugh.

In a work team, the same dynamic applies when we recognize what someone is actually good at and we trust them to do what requires those personal strengths. And, equally important, when we know their strengths and weaknesses, we can keep them away from assignments for which a different kind of personal makeup is needed.

A CEO client of mine had a very gifted CFO. His financial analysis was superb, and he was one of those CFOs who was also a strategic partner. He could do the kind of analysis that got to the real financial drivers of the business and margins that led to great gains. Very talented, and very valuable, in that regard, to have for a CEO.

But, in spite of all of those strong points, my client eventually fired him. Why? Character. Which trait? His inability to be direct and honest with the CEO when there was something the CEO should be doing differently. When he could see that the CEO was going down a wrong path or making a wrong decision, he feared speaking up. He had too much of a need to please. Negative confrontations were hard for him. He could not confront or be direct, and my client needed to be able to trust him to do that.

While certain qualities help make relationships successful and enjoyable and certain ones move businesses forward, there are also traits that get in the way of the trust needed for relationships to go well or business to get done. Here are just a few to consider:

- *Defensiveness*: What happens when you feel you cannot point out a problem to someone or you need them to change a behavior? If they are defensive, conflicts are very difficult to resolve and corrections are a nightmare.

- *Anger*: What is it like to try to trust someone in a close relationship, either personally or in work, who is prone to angry outbursts, rage, or explosiveness? Often it is better not to trust them at all: "Do not make friends with a hot-tempered person, do not associate with one easily angered" (Prov. 22:24 NIV).

- *Narcissism*: Where do we even begin? The narcissistic person's drive to always be seen as wonderful and perfect and ideal wears thin in the best of scenarios. And in other situations, it can become destructive when they feel slighted in any way. They retaliate. Trust is difficult with someone who always has to make it "about them" in some way.

- *Drama and emotional instability*: Trusting someone is difficult when you do not know what kind of theater you will get on any given day. When something goes wrong, an unstable or overly dramatic person can keep anything good from happening. At best, you will gradually just get sick of it, and at worst, you'll be unable to do what you need to do.

- *Control*: Many highly competent, highly qualified people have a strong aggressive drive to get things done and to accomplish a lot. But along with that can come a strong tendency to try to be in control of everything, including possibly you. People who respect other people's boundaries are the types of individuals that are trustworthy, while those who invade people's spaces and try to dictate others' choices are not.

- *Neediness and dependency*: In adulthood, while we all have to depend on each other, some people are overly needy and really can't do a mutual, adult relationship well at all. They need a therapist, not a situation in which someone else is depending on them.

- *Irresponsibility*: As Proverbs says, to depend on an irresponsible person is a nightmare: "Like vinegar to the teeth and smoke to the eyes, so is the slacker to those who send him" (Prov. 10:26 BSB). You depend on them, and then they drop the ball.

- *Codependency or lack of boundaries*: Depending on someone who is unable to say "no" often ends up in something not working. They allow others to take advantage of your resources and time, or they are unable to set limits on people where it affects you and what you are depending on them to do.

- *Gossip or divisive behavior*: Proverbs 17:9 teaches that a gossip "separates close friends" (NIV). And Proverbs 11:13 says, "A gossip betrays a confidence, but a trustworthy person keeps a secret" (NIV). Many personal and professional scenarios are ruined by people who are either divisive or cannot keep a confidence. They can destroy relationships, teams, families, and company cultures.

While this is not a book on character, hopefully just a short list like the one above will make you think about the importance of a person's makeup before you trust them in specific situations. Remember, I am not saying that people with imperfections (other than lying, cheating, or stealing) are not trustworthy; we all have imperfections and issues. What is important, though, is that there is some sort of match in someone's makeup and the areas in which you want to trust that person.

One company I worked with had a very difficult turnaround project that was probably going to take a good two years to get right side up. The person under consideration to run it was very smart and very good at operations. He was a problem solver and a great systems person. He could have brought a lot of horsepower to the situation and created great operations.

But I told them "no."

"Why not?" they asked.

"He is really gifted and competent, but he has too many needs for positive feedback. And this situation is not going to be one that always gives him good feelings about himself like he needs. It is going to be a long, hard dig and there are not going to be a lot of wins or good numbers for a long time. His ego just can't take that, and he will get discouraged and run out of steam. Plus, he has pretty fixed ideas of how everything ought to be and this is going to require a lot of flexibility and adaptability as well. He needs something more stable where he can just do a good job that makes him feel good," were my thoughts.

If the situation were one where things were going smoothly and he could drill down and do a diligent job and get great results and have everyone think he was wonderful, he was the right guy. I had seen him do it many times. But this job was going to need someone with less need for approval, and much thicker skin. Someone who could persevere without a lot of stroking, and that was not him. Intelligence and competency aside, he was not trustworthy for this specific context because he had the wrong makeup for it. Not a good fit.

Think of Character as "Real" Integrity

So what we have seen is that character matters. We have also seen that the word means more than just moral or ethical character. While foundational, and essential, ethics and morality are not enough. "Character that can be trusted for specific situations" is closer to what the word *integrity* really means.

A great definition of *integrity* is the "state of being complete or undivided."* Someone can have moral or ethical character traits, but not be a "complete" or "whole" person in terms of having "integrated" other needed traits into their makeup. In fact, the word *integrity* comes from the same root word from which we get "integer," which means a "whole number." *Wholeness* is the idea here, and we can't rely on someone's honesty to carry the "whole" load of what trustworthiness demands in a particular situation. To truly trust someone, other traits also need to have been integrated into the person's makeup. (See my book *Integrity* for more on wholeness of character in leadership.)

Again, you are not looking for "perfect wholeness of everything it means to be human" in one person, or you would be looking for a long time. But before trusting someone in a particular, specific way—for particular, specific outcomes—make sure there is enough of the

---

* "Integrity," Merriam-Webster, updated November 24, 2022, https://www.merriam-webster.com/dictionary/integrity.

whole picture of traits you need to be able to depend on that person, no matter how honest or brilliant they might be.

We have seen that trustworthiness requires several components, not just one or two. We've looked at understanding, motive, ability, and character. Let's move on to the final essential of trust: track record.

EIGHT

TRACK RECORD:
THE FIFTH ESSENTIAL OF TRUST

Before the iPhone and GPS directions, my wife and I were visiting friends in South Louisiana, way down in Bayou country. We had never been there before and did not know how to get to the event, so I pulled into a little gas station for directions.

"Can you tell me how to get to this restaurant?" I asked the lady at the counter.

"Sure," she said. And proceeded to give me some directions. She said to go down the road a little ways, turn here, and turn there. Then she said something that threw me.

"When you see the big dog lying in the grass, turn right," she said.

What? A big dog lying in the grass? Seriously? That is going to be my road sign?

I questioned her. "Turn when I see the dog? Uh, how will I know this dog is going to be there?" I asked. Seemed a little shaky to me. I felt I needed a road sign that couldn't just get up and chase a cat, leaving me lost.

She was certain. "Yessir, he'll be there, lying in the grass. He's always there. Just turn when you see him," she said.

I didn't know what to say. So, I went back to the car and simply told Tori that I had the directions.

We drove along, making the turns the lady at the gas station told me about. And then, there he was—a German shepherd lying in the grass. I could not believe it. So, I turned there, and we found our event.

What was that? How could the lady have been so certain the dog would be there? Because of one of the most important aspects of trust and our fifth element of trust: the dog had a track record.

He'd been in that same place at that time of day, every afternoon, for years. It was his spot, and he was never not there. You could depend on it.

Track Record Matters

Put yourself in my place again regarding knee surgery. If you were walking to the scheduling desk and saw a body lying in the hallway, with a deep purple look on his face, not moving, you would probably first be startled, and then ask the surgeon, "What the heck is that?"

But then, what if he replied, "Oh, that's a guy I operated on yesterday. That one didn't turn out so well."

At that moment, who cares about how understanding he is, and all of the other essentials of trust we have discussed? This guy just killed someone in a knee surgery. I don't think that happens too often and it is a really bad sign. No trust for him, as vital as they are!

The lesson is this: *what someone has done before is usually the best indicator of what will happen next time.*

The best predictor of the future is the past.

When we trust someone, we place ourselves in a vulnerable position, depending on someone to behave or perform in a certain way. And by definition, if they don't, we will get hurt in some way—emotionally, relationally, financially, or even physically. If we don't know if they are able to come through for our vulnerability, or *especially* if they have never done it before, we are rolling the dice. But if we *know*, based on a track record, that they have performed in a certain way before, the odds go up considerably.

There is good reason for that. Traits and competencies that matter significantly, such as the ones we've been discussing, are not first-time performances or *behaviors that can be done by "choice" or "acts of the will."* This means that someone who has performed poorly or never at all can't just promise, "Oh, I'll change. I'll do it differently this time, I promise." Why? Because, unless something has drastically changed to build new abilities, they are the same person, with the same level of abilities or traits, who failed the last time. They can't just choose to be different. *They have to become different.*

What someone has done before is usually the best indicator of what will happen next time.

The easiest example to understand this is the addict. How many times does a substance abuser or a sex addict, when caught, promise, "I'll stop. I won't do it again"? And spouses or significant others trust that promise. It might even be sincere.

But, the reality is that until the competency for sobriety has been built through recovery, and then demonstrated, the ability is not yet there and trust is not warranted. Certainly, addicts DO change. I have seen it many, many times. They get to a place where they can be trusted. But, trust is going to come *after* they have done some significant work to develop the ability that we are trusting them to have, and they have to establish a significant track record before we put them in a position of trust where they might cause heartache or damage again.

Trust cannot be given only on a promise.

We'll get to more about this in an upcoming chapter, but the point here is that *trust cannot be given only on a promise*. It depends on some abilities, and the only way we know the abilities are there is for them (or similar abilities) to have been demonstrated before. For example, even though Tiger Woods had never played the professional golf tour, Nike trusted him with boatloads of money because he had shown the abilities that would transfer to the PGA.

The point to remember here is that the abilities that we have seen in the first four essentials of trust are not new choices people just make, actions people just take if they have never been able to do them before. A liar doesn't suddenly start always telling the truth. A non-listener does not suddenly choose to be a deep listener who helps others to feel understood. Selfish people don't suddenly start caring about others. Untrained or inexperienced people don't suddenly succeed at complex projects. Lazy people don't suddenly become Energizer bunnies. Addicts don't suddenly break free from established habits.

We need objective reasons to have hope and trust.

People can change but not without a process that both creates the change and displays the new abilities. But to trust someone who has a track record of not being trustworthy just because they promise to do better is not very smart. Where is that new ability going to come from? We need to have seen something tangible first in order to trust. The four trust essentials we have discussed are all achievable for pretty much anyone. People grow and change, but *the only way we know they can actually deliver on these things is for them to prove it. We need objective reasons to have hope and trust.*

Earlier, I mentioned my brother-in-law Mark, the Navy SEAL. Mark was an awesome warrior, husband, father, brother, friend, community member, and American. We lost him in Iraq, killed in battle in 2008. It was a devastating blow to all who loved him and depended on him.

Through hearing so many "Mark stories," as we laughingly called them after he would return from various deployments, here are a few things I know you could trust Mark to be able to do: jump out of an airplane at 30,000 feet in full scuba gear with tanks, descend to the ocean floor and take a nap since he had been up for two days, change into another set of gear, band together with five other SEALs and board an enemy ship in the dark of night, take it down, return it to a holding station, and then have breakfast. No big deal—for them.

He and his teammates could be trusted. But, how did the navy know that?

Track record. SEALs establish a track record before they are sent on a mission.

The process of becoming a SEAL is unmatched in its intensity and difficulty, and very few of the many incredible physical and mental specimens who enter the path to become a SEAL actually make it. Only the most qualified applicants enter the last phase of the process, called BUD/S, and then Hell Week, which is very, very rigorous. Only a small percentage of the "best of the best" make it through Hell Week and can be trusted to be on a SEAL team.

The "magic" of this training, which is in itself a "self-select-out" program, is that basically it is ONLY the ones who can actually finish who become SEALs. In other words, to become a SEAL, you have to show that you can do what battle is going to demand *before* you are sent into dangerous war zones and missions. The navy is not guessing, or hoping. These men have a track record of being able to do what is going to be demanded of them.

A recruit will go through almost impossibly rigorous training and almost unbearable pain before he is ready to be deployed on an actual mission. SEALs are tested and proven.

Yet, in our normal lives, how many people extend trust without knowing and validating someone's track record? How many jump into serious relationships without really knowing someone's relationship history or start businesses with someone who has never started or run a business before?

Validating someone's track record would seem like a no-brainer, right? But we all have trusted people who are unproven, perhaps because of their strengths or their likability or some other great quality. Or worse, we trust someone when their track record is not good and we decide to forgive and trust them anyway and then feel betrayed when they fail.

Fortunately, the navy doesn't just trust without a track record. Nor, as I experienced firsthand, does the air force. I was asked to do some leadership development with the fighter pilots in training at a fighter pilot training facility. Top Gun pilots are the best of the best and will ultimately be entrusted with a critical mission. How does the air force know those pilots will pull it off and deliver on that trust? *Track record.* What I didn't know was that I was going to get to be part of that track record for the group I was working with.

When I was working with these pilots, I was asked to go up in one of the fighter jets so I could really understand what it is they do. I thought, "Awesome! I would love to ride in one of those planes! This will be fun!"

What I didn't realize was that I was not just going on a joy ride or sightseeing tour. I was actually going to ride backseat with one of the training pilots, who had flown many combat missions in his career, in an actual dog fight training where the pilots are trying to shoot each other down and evade being shot down, with everything as real as in an actual air fight, except the actual ammunition ("hits" are registered electronically without actually blowing each other out of the sky). So it is as real as real gets in terms of the flight experience.

I was going to experience rolls, dives, and other maneuvers that could exert up to 8 Gs of force on my untrained body. And what I learned was they had to put me through training for a full day before the ride to learn how to keep blood in my upper body. I also had to wear an anti-G suit that uses bladders to constrict the legs and abdomen to keep the blood in the upper body. This was not going to be just any joy ride. I learned about what those kinds of gravitational forces can do to the body and the brain, and how to make sure the blood stayed in my upper body. I had to be trained to adjust the oxygen flow to my mask when feeling any kind of symptoms, as you only have about ten seconds to adjust it *before your brain won't function well enough to turn the dial.* And how to operate the barf equipment so you don't suck your breakfast back down your windpipe. Lots to think about for a non-pilot psychologist.

The experience was nothing short of incredible. What those planes and pilots can do is mind-boggling. But the G forces were harrowing. It was the worst physical experience, apart from abject pain, that I have ever encountered. It was horrible and exhilarating all at once. And my mind was doing all it could to stay present, aware, focused, and think through what I needed to do. And, it just simply would not work at moments. The force was too much.

While I was trying to hold on to consciousness, the pilot was operating an extremely complex machine, reading all sorts of flight and warfare gauges and screens, communicating with his teammates, firing artillery at his enemy, and doing evasive maneuvers to keep from getting blown out of the sky, and many other tasks. And he was doing all this while being under the same amount of body- and brain-defying G forces that I was.

That is the point here about track record. The pilot told me that when a new trainee starts fighter pilot training, they have to go on about forty ride-along flights like I did before they can function well enough to fly the plane. From there, they fly multiple missions a day until the air force is not guessing when they trust them enough to be sent into battle. They *know*. The pilots have a proven track record.

(By the way, my pilot told me he had taken five civilians up in his career and I was the only one who didn't either pass out or lose his breakfast. I have to brag a little!)

Trust Is Incremental, and Earned

Trust is not a toggle switch with two settings: on or off. *But, unfortunately, that's how many people view it.* They meet or even know someone, then in some arena, either personal or professional, go from no trust (because it is a new relationship or the context for trust is new) to total trust. Think about a person who decides to marry after three or four dates, or a company that promotes a new hire to department head after a few months of employment. These situations often don't end well because people haven't been required to prove themselves.

Trust is not simply given, it's earned.

Trust is not simply given, it's earned. People must show us they are worthy of it, and that only happens through incremental performance over time. Time, not just performance, is a big factor here, and unfortunately, too many people are impatient. They base their trust on their impressions or judgments and not on objective data, which track record provides.

Although we are talking about time you personally experience with someone, that is not always necessary. A person can have a great track record over time but you were not involved in it. That's fine. It's what a great résumé or reputation is about. You don't have to have played on a team with Tom Brady to trust him with a football. But, not being part of someone's history does not negate that building a track record took time. Time is still a factor, even if you were not there.

So, if you are beginning a new relationship, or entrusting more to an existing relationship, make sure that there is a track record of objective performance on which to base your trust, even if you didn't witness it personally.

Family businesses often, unfortunately, provide examples of what can happen when trust is bestowed without the benefit of a track record. Positions of high rank are given simply because someone is a family member, without deference to that person possessing the skills and competencies required of the role and with no history of performance. Many great family businesses require family members to work somewhere else for a few years, earn some promotions, then come back to the family business once they have proven themselves.

Be Forewarned

Track records are so important and powerful that they can even be used to lull very smart people into bad trust decisions. Think Bernie Madoff. His track record, or people's belief in his track record, basically made his scandal possible.

Many Ponzi schemes actually pay returns, building a track record. People trust it because we are wired to trust what we see. Yet, it's a sham. When people asked their friends about their experience with Bernie, the friends said, "We're getting great returns! It is so good!" The potential investors believe their friends, because they're getting paid, even though it is *deceptive*. The returns are fake, but it is a track record of being "paid."

Track records matter. How else could Bernie Madoff have run away with sixty-five billion dollars of very smart people's money? Again, the reason is that we are wired that way. Our brains develop maps that enable us to negotiate reality. When you walk to the kitchen in the morning to make your coffee, you depend on a map your brain has made. Go downstairs, take a left, walk five steps, and take a right. You can trust the kitchen to be there. The map has been built over several trips of going to the kitchen, and it has a track record of working. This is why we bump into walls in hotels getting up in the middle of the night going to the bathroom. There is either no map or our brain is operating on the map from home. We need accurate maps, but either way, your brain is building them based on experience and then executes according to the map. We trust our brain maps and we act accordingly.

Track records align with how we are wired. Our brains negotiate life based largely on what happened "last time." So, other than in the case of Ponzi track records, you are well served to value track records. Ponzi schemes are out there, so we must vet the track records, of course. But we should always look for them, demand them, and value them.

You Build Maps for Other People

When we are trying to build trust in others, we must be aware that we are always building a map, a track record, in someone's head. That map will make them able to trust us, or not. Here is how it works, every day.

Let's say someone has an issue, a problem, a difficulty, and they reach out to their boss for help. They go talk to the boss, lay out their dilemma, and the boss listens well and gives valuable input and support. It was a "transformational moment," transforming someone from a confused or discouraged state of being, to a state of clarity and motivation. It went well. Or if they were feeling a little doubtful of the strategy, unsure enough to move forward, the conversation explained the reasons well enough that they got back to fully being on board. They were "transformed" from one state to another.

The next time that team member needs help, she will be more apt to request a one-on-one with the boss. Why? It went so well last time. The boss builds greater trust with each interaction, as each one builds on the "went well last time" map. Every experience with someone adds to that map of "how it went the last time."

If we were always aware that we are building a map, and aware of what happened last time, how would it affect the way we interact with our spouses, employees, families, customers, church and community leaders, and others? We'd realize how much track records matter in all of life.

Problems Are Not a Problem, But Patterns Are

Again, every interaction we have builds a track record. We all make mistakes, and most mistakes can be overcome, especially when a long track record proves the mistake is an anomaly. Obviously some mistakes are huge and that's a different matter. But overall, humans make mistakes. We miss things and make errors. The big question with mistakes is: Does it validate the map or is it seen as just an error in the map?

Let's say that Brittany is a stellar member of your team, or even a friend in your personal life. She follows through on commitments. You can depend on her. You can trust her, like the German shepherd in the grass.

One day, you have all agreed to meet at a certain time and place. You are all there, except Brittany. After about fifteen minutes, people begin to say things like, "Someone call Brittany. Maybe she's sick or her car broke down." Her mistake broke her pattern, so it must be seen as an anomaly because Brittany is always dependable. She has a track record. No one is upset with Brittany. In fact, they're concerned about her. Because she has high trust.

Compare Brittany to Jason. He's affable and smart. Everyone loves him, but they view him as a "flake." He's rarely on time and sometimes misses appointments altogether. If he's late for something, no one waits for him. The map he's built for them has taught them not to.

That is how maps work. And in relation to building trust, we never can overestimate their power because the brain is wired to build them. In fact, they're so powerful, that once one is built, overcoming the perception of it can be difficult. It takes specific work, which we'll discuss later in the book. Suffice it to say here that we are much better off building a good map instead of needing to repair an old one that is not so good. Track record matters.

I teach that problems are normal, and everyone makes mistakes. The thing to do when you make a mistake is to address it and fix it. Own it, put your arms around what caused it, and make sure it doesn't happen again. Problems will not ruin what you are doing, unless in some instances they are too big and arise too early.

But if you do not address a problem and it does happen again, you no longer have a problem. Now you have a pattern—an established way of operating. And patterns will kill you. They are like water that continues to run out of a drain across the same patch of dirt, forming a stream that continues to flow. Patterns repeat themselves. They are like mutations in DNA, and when the DNA mutates, then it becomes a new identity. When a bad pattern develops, for example, a company becomes "the one that always misses deadlines," not the "company that missed *a* deadline." Those are very different. One is a problem, the other is a pattern. And that pattern has become an identity. The team lost a game vs. the team is a losing team.

Whether the patterns are yours or someone else's, be keenly aware of them because, like Brittany and Jason, they enable you to predict behavior. Whether they are good or bad, maps, patterns, and track records are trustworthy.

Temptations to Skip the Track Record

One reason people make poor decisions about trusting others is that they think they can excuse or overlook someone's track record. I'll delve into this later in the book, but here I simply want to mention two dynamics that can cause people to believe someone has a good track record when they don't.

"I'm Sorry"

Recognizing the importance of a track record is often easier in the initial season of trusting someone than it is later, because new relationships, or the possibility of trusting in a new way in an existing relationship, puts you in evaluation mode. Nothing bad has happened yet. The idea of trust is still hypothetical. So, you are evaluating.

But what about a relationship, personal or professional, in which a trust failure has already occurred or a breach of trust is ongoing? It is easy to see the need for a "necessary ending" when there is a clear bad track record and no change in sight. However, that is not what always happens. Sometimes, there is a poor track record, and someone confronts the person, or threatens a firing or a divorce, and suddenly the person "sees the light." They are sorry, pleading, repentant, committed to "never doing it again." And the plea is for forgiveness and to allow them to have another chance.

Where there is great love, or history, or attachment, or even need, the wish and the hope and the temptation is to forgive what has happened, embrace their sincerity to change, and to wipe the slate clean and go forward. Forgive the past and extend trust for the future.

Many times—*wrong*. Certainly mistakes can be forgiven and we just get back on track. But if the breach is egregious, then usually not requiring some sort of process before trusting again is a bad idea.

We discussed this earlier in the need for new activities to be building a new track record. No need to reiterate it, but I did feel the need to emphasize one point: "I'm sorry" is not enough for trust. It may be enough to open the door to a conversation about how trust can be restored, but it is not enough to automatically trust and move forward.

An apology, confession, repentance—all are essential for "forgiveness." But they are not good reasons to trust someone in the future. Trust must be earned, as I've noted, by an incremental track record of being engaged in a process of change and a track record of incremental growth and success. They must show you that they have changed.

The issue here is this: do not get sucked in to trust because of the sincerity of "I'm sorry." It may be offered in the utmost sincerity. It may be golden and beautiful and lead to all sorts of forgiveness, healing, and reconciliation. But to go from there to automatic trust, believing everything will be different, may not be wise. Trust for the future must be earned as a track record for success is built.

Trust by Association

Another instance that tempts people not to look deeply enough into someone's track record is when that person has a halo effect because of their association with someone else. I mentioned Bernie Madoff earlier, and he is a good example of trust by association. Some people trusted him because of a deceptive track record, but others trusted him because they thought, *If so-and-so is investing with him, he must be legit. He must be trustworthy and dependable. This must be good.* Wrong.

In fact, this dynamic was so powerful that the Kellogg School of Management at Northwestern University studied it specifically. As the researchers put it: "Our research suggests that Madoff may have deliberately or inadvertently taken advantage of the automatic trust process regardless of whether his family members and business associates were victims or confederates. *Even if he didn't seem trustworthy, the fact that his closest relatives and associates invested with him could have provided a subtle, nonconscious signal that he was actually trustworthy.* After all, foxes never prey near their dens, and thieves only steal far from their homes. *Additionally, the constant associations of Madoff's name with all sorts of philanthropic works, and other subtle cues, may also have encouraged people to trust when they shouldn't have."*

And then, "Put simply, our findings suggest that trust may not always develop via an incremental, evaluative process. Social and relational cues may have a strong but subtle impact on people's important financial and management choices. Understanding the nonconscious nature of this process can help you take advantage of its benefits while avoiding its downsides—and avoiding the next Bernie Madoff, too."**

We often trust people based on a referral, or an association. And those are *very important.* They can validate someone's abilities, *as long as they include the knowledge of a real track record in the way that we are going to trust them.* The one who is connected to the person we are going to trust may have a relationship with them, but *may never have had to depend on them in the way we are thinking about trusting them.* They may never had been in a position to evaluate what we are trusting the person to do. They just know and like them. That's not a good reason to trust.

Here is a common example of this scenario: You have a great single friend. Lovely person. Successful, friendly, accomplished. So you set this person up with another single friend, thinking, "They are both such wonderful people. This is going to be great."

---

* Li Huang and J. Keith Murnighan, "Why Everybody Trusted Madoff," *Forbes*, December 22, 2010, https://www.forbes.com/2010/12/22/bernard-madoff-trust-psychology-leadership-managing-ponzi.html?sh=4ea62e81de90.

** Huang and Murnighan, "Why Everybody Trusted Madoff."

The two begin to date and get serious. Everything looks good until . . . it doesn't. One of them, as wonderful a friend as they may be, turns out to be a nightmare in romantic relationships. Controlling, jealous, clingy, or abusive even. Behaviors that were never seen *in a different context as friends become central, and devastating, in the dating/ romance relationship.* Context really matters when it comes to track record.

Or, someone is vying for your business in a particular arena. Everything looks good and they give another person you know and respect as a reference. You are impressed. "Well if they know so-and-so, and she or he will vouch for them, then they must be great. I'll call them to get the go-ahead," you think. Then you make the call and the friend of yours is effusive about the other person's great qualities. They absolutely love them, can't say enough good things.

The problem is that your friend has never done business with them. There is no track record in that arena. Yet, because of the halo effect of the friend, you believe the person has to be great, and you go forward without really knowing what you need to know. Sometimes this can be a very big mistake. Good in one context of a relationship does not necessarily mean good in another.

What Happened Last Time?

There is an old saying: "Fool me once, shame on you. Fool me twice, shame on me." This isn't always true, but it's true often enough. Anyone can get duped, scammed, or victimized. Bad people do happen to good people. No way to see it coming at times.

But once we have seen a pattern on someone or experienced a breach of trust, we need to be careful. Ignore a track record is often to our folly. As Proverbs says, "The prudent see danger and take refuge, but the simple keep going and pay the penalty" (Prov. 27:12 NIV). Once we see the danger, it is prudent to be careful before trusting again.

Even if we have no experience with someone, we can still see the danger, or the success if we are diligent enough to demand for ourselves a real track record before we go forward. The best predictor of the future is the past, in most cases or unless there is some intervening event or variable to ensure a better future.

Again, this does not mean at all that we cannot trust someone in a new position or context they've never been in before. Otherwise, there would be no such thing as promotions, first-time CEOs, or recipients of investment. Every single person who becomes engaged to be married for the first time is in this scenario. No problem that they have "never done *this* before." They don't have a track record in marriage. But they can have a track record of the kinds of qualities and capabilities that can transfer to the marriage context. And if we look for track record—in every situation in life—we'll be on surer footing than we will if we don't.

Putting It to Work

There you have them, the five essentials of trust:

1. Understanding
2. Motive
3. Ability
4. Character
5. Track Record

Trust is multidetermined, meaning that it has several components. Having one or two of them doesn't mean we automatically hit the "trust" button. We need all five when we trust in significant areas of life with significant risk.

We have also seen that we do not need to look for perfection. We need to trust people in their lanes of strength. No one will have all essentials of trust to perfection in every context of life. We can trust certain people in some ways but not so much in others. That's okay too. I'm not asking all of my friends to be my knee surgeon. They can still be good friends or business partners as long as I am not depending on them to do something they are not good at.

Each essential of trust can be vetted by checking into a person's track record over time. People can fake something temporarily in order to get what they want. But it is difficult to sustain a charade for a longer time, especially when they are not yet getting everything they want.

Now that you have seen the five building blocks and know what to look for, let's look at what is required from the *other* side.

We need to trust people in their lanes of strength.

THREE

GROWING IN TRUST

NINE

BUILD YOUR TRUST MUSCLE

John and Sean started their business together as best friends and colleagues. It was difficult in the beginning, as most startups are, but they persevered. They survived several close calls involving running out of cash, facilities becoming unavailable, difficulties in staffing, and other issues that had them teetering near the precipice of failure at times, but they made it through them all. In the fourth year, finally, things were really going well. The company was building quite a brand and had a strong following, and they were making more money than either of them ever thought they would. Success was a reality.

Their success brought with it opportunities, as success often does. Several outside entities approached them, offering to buy the company. At first, they had no interest in selling, but as time went on, the inquiries increased, and eventually became too significant to ignore. Serious venture and private equity firms pressed John and Sean pretty hard. They began to get interested in making a deal and the talks grew more serious.

Finally, with a firm from the Silicon Valley, they got past the exploration stages and began actually negotiating specifics of a potential deal. This group had experience in taking many businesses public and had done very well. They were seasoned and respected. Sean and

John's advisers, families, and friends said they would be fools to not go forward with the deal. Gradually, John began to agree and ultimately reached the point where he was ready to sell.

The more they talked, the more uneasy Sean became. Nothing was wrong with the deal, the terms, or the people, though. Everything was good in that regard. Still, Sean was hesitant to move forward and sell the company. Slowly, his reticence became an issue between him and John. One wanted to go forward and the other did not. John worked hard to push Sean down the road toward "yes," but the closer they got to a deal, the more he began to shut down.

At this point, Sean and I talked. I could see the opportunity and understand why he and John should sell. It made total business sense. I couldn't see why he wouldn't want to move forward. He was tired of the toll running the business had taken, and this would provide some needed air to breathe. Selling would give him more money than he had ever thought possible in many ways and allow him to devote the time and attention the business had taken for the past four years to his young family. It seemed like a great reward for all he had done.

"So, why don't you want to do this?" I asked.

"It just doesn't feel good," he said. "I don't know why, but it just doesn't."

From there, I began exploring some possible reasons selling the company felt uncomfortable to him. Increasingly, his reluctance seemed more psychological than business oriented.

Did he not want to lose the close working relationship between just him and his buddy, John? Was he afraid of losing the intimacy of a closely held team to a larger group? Was he struggling to let go of the excitement and infatuation of the startup season and having a hard time moving to becoming a "real" company? Did he simply want things to keep going as they'd always been? Would he just be longing for the past?

As we explored his feelings, it became apparent that he was wrestling with two issues: the first was losing control, and the second was being accountable to an external board. We began discussing these issues, and he asked good questions. All the issues he raised were solvable. He and Sean would have board seats, they could limit their roles in ways that worked for them, and the deal would allow for other things I thought should be positive for Sean. But still, the reticence.

Finally, Sean's voice began to crack and his chin began to quiver. I asked him what he was feeling.

He almost couldn't get the words out of his mouth. "I just hate it. I hate the thought of answering to them and their telling us what we have to do, how to do it—like the company is theirs and not ours. *This is my life! Not theirs!*" he said with intense emotion.

We sat in silence for a moment. I asked him, "Have you ever felt this feeling before? Does it remind you of anything?"

He sat quietly and then softly began to cry. I asked what was happening.

"I don't want to live in someone else's world—in their house, not mine."

"House?"

"Yes. Like they dictate everything and I have no choices, no voice. I can't do it. I can't," he said.

"Is this a familiar feeling? Have you felt this way before?" I asked.

"My old man was like that. I won't ever live under that kind of control again. I won't do it. We can go out of business before I will let someone tell me how I am going to live my life and make my choices," he said. "This is *mine*, not theirs. This is *my* company and *my* life."

"Wow. That must feel terrible," I said. "Tell me about life at your house with your dad."

Then he unloaded, and what he shared truly was awful. He told me about his life growing up with a dictatorial father, and it was nothing any of us would want. Without going into detail, to say he was micromanaged and controlled is an understatement. And for Sean, that was what the business deal represented—living under authoritarian control, being micromanaged in a way that diminished even what it meant to be a person. Just like life with Dad. No way was he going to do this.

We talked more about Sean's situation, in several more conversations—just Sean and me, with John, and with the investors. We spoke of the core issues for Sean: He could not trust the group to live up to their promises. He still believed he would experience a total loss of control and loss of his life as he knew it. We talked about how this would be a contractual business relationship with clear boundaries, and we looked at the potential buyers' track record of investments with other startups and at how well those were going. We went through many scenarios that did everything but perfectly guarantee Sean what he wanted and enrich his whole life in many ways. Actually, the arrangement would have given him much more freedom than he said he wanted.

But we never got there. He could not trust anyone in a relationship that felt like they had any kind of authority over him. He couldn't agree to be accountable to a larger entity. He simply could not trust an authority relationship at all.

The deal went away. And ultimately so did his relationship with John to the degree that they still had a relationship, as his fears of being controlled and lack of trust increased and flowed into how they ran the business. Ultimately, he got out of the business altogether and started another one on his own.

Good decision? No one thought so, except Sean. But he got what he wanted:

> "I will not trust anyone to have any authority over me. I will do it myself, even if it means being 'by myself.'"

Choosing to Take the Risk

In section 1 of this book, we outlined a model of trust. We looked at the five essentials that put us in a safe enough place to take the risk of trust so we might gain the benefits of trust.

At the same time, there is *always* risk. Trust, by many definitions, refers to entering into a state of vulnerability with the potential of being hurt.

We still have to choose to take the step to trust, and it always entails risk.

As we have seen, all good things in life come from trusting "another," whether the "other" is an individual, such as a marriage partner, or a group, such as a corporate board or a group of investors. This is because trust is the vehicle through which we receive what we need. Our trust model—the five essentials of trust—helps us make the decision to trust well. But there is another issue at hand: no matter how much the other person or entity looks trustworthy, *we still have to choose to take the step to trust, and it always entails risk.* The model helps us figure out how to minimize risk, for sure. But usually, there are no guarantees.

We see, then, that trust always involves *two* parties in order to be trust: *you* and the person you are trusting. It's a relationship. We can evaluate the other party in wise ways and make informed choices about them. We can choose and vet the other person or group. And they can actually be "trustworthy." But *there are always two parties. You are part of the equation as well. It is never only about the other person and their trustworthiness. It is always about both of us: the "other" and "me."*

Are You the Problem?

The fact that trust involves two entities invites us to assess how good we are at trust. How well do we do it? Do we have anything to do with a breakdown in trust? Or in the ability to trust? Someone can be trustworthy, yet we may not be able to trust them. This is because trust issues are not always on the other side of a relationship. *Sometimes we stand in the way of trust;* our issues—not theirs—are the problem. I call this having a broken trust muscle, and it's important for us to examine and understand why trust muscles break down. We need to look at ourselves in relation to trust issues just as carefully as we look for the essentials of trust we need to see in other people.

Someone can be trustworthy, but if I am limited in my ability to trust, I will miss out on a lot of life. Not because others are not trustworthy, *but because I cannot trust very well because of my own issues with trust.* We sometimes hear that certain people have "trust issues," meaning that their "trust muscle" needs to be repaired, healed, or even built for the first time. And when we say that, it is usually talking about there being a problem caused by the "trust issues."

Trust issues can destroy a person's life.

Trust issues can destroy a person's life. Sean's inability to trust cost him millions of dollars, the life he had been working toward, and his relationship with John. Every day, people can move away from or even blow up relationships and businesses because they lack the ability to trust a person or an entity. Much can be at stake—including marriages, family, friendships, work teams, deals, the ability to join a church or group, and other important things—if people cannot restore their ability to trust. Remember, trust is the key to life, and the way to have a full life is not only to find trustworthy people, but to be able to enter into relationships with them well.

Your Trust Muscle

You didn't think you would go through an entire book written by a psychologist without going back to childhood, did you? Sorry. But as Sean discovered, sometimes we have to see that the issue we are dealing with in the present may not be about the present at all. It could be about something we bring from the past *into the present situation*. Trust is like that.

Many people resist this idea, believing that the past is over and done. In one sense, they're right. We can't go back into the past unless we have a time machine. But reality is that we don't have to go back into the past. We continually bring the past into today. It's right in front of us, both good and bad. In Sean's case, the old unresolved trust issue that developed in his relationship with his father was not in the past at all. It was acted out right in front of our eyes, in the present.

There really is not as much mystery to this stuff about the past as some people would like you to believe. Look at it this way. You are driving your car, you get rear-ended, and the axle gets bent. The accident happened on a certain day last year. But you have two cars, so you just leave the damaged one at home and start driving the other one. A year later, a friend borrows your spare car, so you decide to drive the one with the bent axle, thinking, *Maybe it's not as messed up as I thought. I can drive it for a few days.*

You take it out, and within a few miles the vibration is just too bad to continue, even as a backup. Having no other option, you take it into the shop. The mechanic asks you about the symptoms, checks it out, and says, "You have a bent axle. We'll have to fix it before this car is ever going to be normal. How did this happen?"

"Oh, about a year ago, I got rear-ended and just never got it fixed. I've been driving my other car instead, but today I had to use this one," you explain.

"Well, that's in the past so that shouldn't matter. I don't believe in all of that 'past' garbage. People blame their bad cars on their past all the time. Seems like a cop-out to me. Today is today, so just forget what happened yesterday and drive the car. What do you think I am, a psychiatrist?"

You would look at the repairman as though he's crazy. You *know* the past is affecting today. It does not matter whether the axle got bent a year ago or yesterday or today. The damage is real. The axle is bent, and until it is addressed, the car won't be drivable.

A similar dynamic is true for people. Our lives are comprised first of all of the developmental experiences in our growing up years. This is like the car being built in the factory. Babies come into the world with no ability to have a secure attachment, the most basic ability to trust another person and depend on them without fear. They have the *potential* to trust and feel secure, but it must be developed into an *ability*. In the "factory" of the early years of bonding and attachment, the ability to trust securely is built. That ability is a piece of equipment that we carry around inside for the rest of our lives, like the parts of a car.

People who develop a strong ability to trust through secure early relationships do well later in other relationships.

When someone develops the ability to trust and maintain a secure attachment with a trustworthy "other," that ability is what I am referring to as the "trust muscle." It is the equipment inside of us, like an axle on a car, that enables us to trust. It is our trust machine. If it works well, we trust well. People who develop a strong ability to trust through secure early relationships do well later in other relationships. All the research in the world has proven that, as does Psalm 22:9: "Yet you brought me safely from my mother's womb and led me to trust you at my mother's breast" (NLT). We learn trust very, very early in life.

Trust Muscles Can Be Installed and Repaired

But what if, personally speaking, someone has a wreck? What if their axle gets bent? Or broken? What if it was never installed to begin with? Then, that equipment—their trust muscle—is broken. They carry the inability to trust well within themselves, just as the person who carries a healthy trust muscle carries the capacity to trust.

When someone with a damaged or missing trust muscle tries to use it, to drive the car down a normal road such as a relationship or a business deal, so to speak, the car begins to vibrate, or not work at all, or even steer itself into a ditch. In other words, their being malfunctions and they can't get where they need to go in life. Sort of like what happened to Sean. His deal ended up in the ditch.

When psychologists speak of dealing with past issues that are unresolved, they are talking about fixing what has been broken and carried around unrepaired for years and making it so it can work again. Until the repair happens, people live out their trust issues in relationship after relationship, or situation after situation, repeating the patterns of not being able to trust and suffering the consequences. They inflict those consequences on other people as well. This is what Sean did. He lived out an old battle in the present, and he hurt himself and others in the process.

Saying that we have trust issues that are rooted in the past is like saying we have the flu. We probably caught it yesterday, or sometime before this moment. But just as we can't go back to the time you

caught it and avoid catching it or heal it, we can't go back to someone's personal past to fix a trust issue. And, thankfully, like the flu,
we don't have to go back in the past; we simply have to address and
fix what happened in the past.

Trust muscles can be repaired. An old issue that replays itself in
someone's life can be healed in the present. Had Sean been open, he
could have gotten over his dad's mistreatment, and it would not have
continued to cause him to fear authority and accountability. He could
have realized that other people in authority are different than his dad.
He could have learned to notice how he misinterpreted the present
because of his past and developed some new responses and other skills
that would have changed his life. This would have occurred in the
present with some good help, but it did have roots in the past.

Not recognizing how we taint the present and distort it based
on our past experience is the essence of failing to learn and grow.
At some point, we do well to learn: "Yes, it was cold in January and
you needed that overcoat. Now it is June, and you'd feel better if you
took it off." We no longer need the defensive behaviors against trust
that we learned in the past. Instead, we need to learn to grow "past
our past." We need new skills, and new trust equipment, which can
be built in new, more secure relationships.

How many times have you seen a wonderful new boss heal wounds
inflicted by a not-so-great boss by building a different, more trustworthy relationship with an employee? In such situations, there is a
process involved. It may be rocky in the beginning, as the employee
slowly learns to get past their past and begins to respond differently
in the present because of a new healing relationship. This is how great
teachers, coaches, bosses, mentors, and others are able to be incredible healing forces in our lives, restoring out ability to trust—if we
can let them.

But, before we can get better at trusting, meaning to build our
trust muscle, we have to understand the issues that get in the way of

trust. Emotional and relational injuries from our developing years and even from later relationships break our ability to trust. We need to learn what issues cause us to believe that even trustworthy people are untrustworthy for us, as Sean did. Those issues are our internal, personal barriers to trust. In the next two chapters, let's look at some of the most common ones.

TEN

BREAKING YOUR TRUST BARRIERS, PART 1

We have said that trust is basically making oneself vulnerable to another, with the possibility of being hurt in some way. As in other areas of life, if we are *already* hurt from yesterday, we tend to fear getting too close to using the part of us that hurts, lest we get wounded again. After my knee surgery, I was very careful to not let anyone bump against my leg. The pain was excruciating when that happened, so I stayed clear of getting too close. Similarly, if you get sunburned over the weekend, you steer clear of anyone who might slap you on the shoulders to say hello on Monday at the office. We are already vulnerable enough.

In this chapter and the next one, we'll look at some of the most common fears and issues people walk around with, fears and issues that can serve as barriers to easily trusting another person.

Fear of Depending on Someone

Trust is basically dependency. We depend on someone to come through for us on some promise or expectation. We make ourselves vulnerable with the expectation that they will provide something good for us and not hurt us in the process, either by not coming through or by injuring us in some way.

Our first lessons in trust take place in our early relationships and environments. As the psalmist says, we first learn to depend "at my mother's breast" (Ps. 22:9 NLT), or at our caretaker's bottle. Babies slowly develop security as they learn from experience that their needs will be met. First, someone will respond to their hunger with food. Second, someone will respond to their distress with emotional support and nurture. And third, when they are in pain, someone will bring relief. When they express a need, through crying, frowning, or other signals, and the environment responds, they learn to *depend on others. They learn that needing is a good thing.* As the cycle of need and response repeats itself, the infant gets stronger and grows. And the trust muscle grows as well.

Trust is basically dependency.

But, all our developmental equipment is not alike. We all have different experiences, and some end up more secure than others. These experiences can lead to different kinds of attachment styles. While there are various names given to these by various researchers, I find these descriptions to be helpful:

The Secure Attachment Style
What I've just described in the good scenario above is referred to as a "secure attachment style." People who are equipped with this attachment style tend to be capable of uninterrupted attachments to others later in life because their equipment is solid and in place. They move toward others when they need something, with the expectation that others will be there for them. They are consistent in their trusting relationships and depend on others very well.

On the other hand, when a little person has great needs that are not responded to well, they learn a different lesson: "I can't depend on anyone. The outside world has nothing for me." They withdraw and detach from needing others, developing a "solo" style. When they do depend on others, they act out great fears, which gets in the way of having functional trusting relationships with others. Their relationships are riddled with disruptions as they try to avoid vulnerability or act out the fears that come from an inability to trust another person.

The Anxious Attachment Style

If people have what is called an anxious attachment style, they fear abandonment and can be needy or clingy. They constantly need to be reassured because they feel that others do not care enough about them, won't respond adequately to them, or may reject them. Always fearful, the vulnerability they bring into a relationship causes much distortion and interruption of trust. If someone doesn't text them back promptly, respond to an email soon enough, or doesn't act like a cheerleader for them, they view these behaviors through a lens of fear. Then the connection between the two of them suffers as they act out that fear through dysfunctional behavior.

I have seen business negotiations suffer when one side doesn't respond quickly enough to the other. The side waiting for a response then becomes anxious and acts out by chasing the deal in a needy way that weakens their position or causes it to sour.

Similarly, I have seen romantic relationships get totally blown up as a couple becomes closer and more vulnerability develops. The one with the fear begins to act out his or her fear of abandonment through misinterpretations, clingy behavior, rage, or some other unwarranted behavior. Even worse, that person may simply end the relationship for no reason at all. This is often called "commitment phobia."

I remember a couple who had a great dating relationship, a great connection, and what looked like a great future. Until he proposed.

She accepted, and he *never called her back again*. Literally. Their friends had to intervene to explain to her what had happened. He was so afraid of trusting her in the commitment of marriage, unconsciously terrified that he would be abandoned, that he abandoned her first. He proposed, gave her a ring, left for home that night, and never called her back. And he was a high-level executive. You never know what a broken trust muscle will cause people to do.

The Avoidant Attachment Style

In addition to the secure attachment style and the anxious attachment style, there is the avoidant style. People who operate this way fear getting close to others and trusting them. As a defense, they remain distant. Often, they fear feeling suffocated as they grow closer to someone, and they make sure they don't get close enough to be too vulnerable. Other people experience them as emotionally distant or unavailable as they keep their distance. Others also feel that those with the avoidant style do not meet their needs in the relationship, and they often feel these people ignore them.

The Fearful-Avoidant Attachment Style

There is also the fearful-avoidant style. People in this category want a trusting connection with others, but they avoid it at the same time. They can be chaotic in the way they act this out—craving trust and closeness with others, while simultaneously moving away from them. This particular inability to trust is often associated with other dysfunctional behaviors and can be difficult to deal with from the other side.

What's confusing about this is that often, in the beginning of a relationship, people with this avoidant style can be charming and come on strong. They can be social and seem to want to connect. Then, as they feel vulnerable, they distance themselves. People around them become confused, asking themselves, "What went wrong? What did I do?" In both personal and work relationships, the avoidant can lose a lot and cause much chaos, pain, and drama, as they fail to trust people who are actually quite trustworthy.

In each attachment style we've looked at, what is fascinating to remember is that the five essentials of trust begin with "understanding." We trust when we feel someone really understands what we need, who we are, what hurts us, what helps us, and other things that are important to us. Understanding is the most foundational element of trust.

The amazing part of this is that, from infancy, what is central to a baby's ability to develop trust is the caregiver's understanding, *the ability to read the infant's cues and respond to them appropriately.* For example, the mother or caretaker must be able to understand whether a cry means, "I'm hungry," or "I'm tired." The infant needs them to recognize when a cry says, "I'm upset, and I need to be held and nurtured." Good mothers or caretakers "know" their babies, and later their children. They know what the need is, even before the child has words to articulate it. They understand the child. Our greatest need, from the womb to the tomb, is to be known and understood. Good spouses, friends, business partners, and family "know" each other's needs and respond. In this way, our basic needs never change: we need understanding throughout life.

But when one person gets the cue, or fear, that someone else is not understanding them, that's when suspicion and other forms of brokenness affect the trust muscle. This is why feeling understood is the foundation of all things "trust." When someone has not felt understood during their developing years, they expect that others will not understand what they need, they have a weak trust muscle, and they fear trusting relationships. When this happens in someone's life, they struggle to depend on others, because experience has taught them that depending on people leads to disappointment, unmet needs, or abandonment. They view every situation as a scary opportunity to be hurt again. And worse than that, they have a *confirmation bias to interpret everyone's behavior as untrustworthy*. When someone does not respond immediately, or in the way they view as right, they immediately think, *I knew it. I can't depend on anyone. I'm all on my own.* This is sad, but it's the way their trust muscle works until it gets repaired. Bent axle, all over again.

Many romantic relationships are destroyed by the inability to depend on someone. A couple may do well and their relationship may have many great aspects to it—until real dependency begins to develop. Then, the one who can't trust decides the other person just isn't what they want. And they move on. In reality, there was *nothing* wrong with the other person. Moving on was simply a defensive maneuver. The one with a broken trust muscle had to begin to find something wrong with the other person so they could move away from trust. The same dynamic happens in business relationships. One person finds something wrong with the company, team, partners, boss, customer, or something. They'll find any kind of problem in order to avoid getting close to others and trusting them.

Fear of Being Controlled

We saw from Sean's story how the fear of being controlled works and how powerful it can be. To understand why this is true, we have to look at the building of the trust muscle during the developmental years. Basically, the issue here is one of freedom, specifically the ability to experience oneself as a free person in a relationship. This is a normal developmental building block for human beings. Our first task is to emotionally connect with others, as infants and little children learn and as we discussed earlier.

But what happens next? The toddler years! And toddlers send a strong, clear message:

"You *cannot* control me!"

After we learn to depend on others, the next task we learn in life is how to depend on others *while also being free from those people.* What we communicate at this stage of development is: "Just because I need you and am connected to you does not mean I am giving you total control of me!" We want to be able to be connected to people and have our needs met in the context of trusting them, but we don't want to give up all of our freedom and autonomy just because we are connected to someone.

The fact that people are connected does not mean that one person controls the other, leaving him or her with no choices.

Think of a marriage relationship. It should involve a huge amount of connection and interdependency, but neither person should feel controlled by the other. Each one should feel they still have the freedom to make their own choices, have their own space, pursue their own interests, and the like. The fact that people are connected does not mean that one person controls the other, leaving him or her with no choices. The fear of being controlled and losing freedom can be a *huge* barrier to trust.

Many people have found that they can have a relationship, or they can have freedom, but they can't have both.

Sean was trapped by the fear of being controlled. His story took place in a business environment, but the inability to trust because one fears the loss of freedom leads to personal relationship failures as well, in many ways. I worked with a young man who had a pattern of falling in love with very good women. As the two of them grew closer, he ended up bailing out of the relationship. He earned the label of having a "commitment phobia." People in his circles, people who loved him, advised women to stay away from him. They had seen his track record and knew his history of getting close to several wonderful women, only to break up for reasons that seemed lame.

It was clear that he had no fears of intimacy or being emotionally close. He did that—the "connecting" part—very well. He could be open and vulnerable. But as soon as the relationship reached the point where mutual decisions were needed, such as negotiating how time and energy would be spent, which always call for some amount of sacrifices and the normal giving up of freedoms a relationship requires, he was out the door. If she wanted to spend an afternoon together, and it might cut into his plans to play golf with his buddies or pursue some other individual interest, he would suddenly begin to shut down emotionally and want out of the relationship. He had no idea that negotiations and compromises were possible, that each person could enjoy freedoms while still being committed to the other. He didn't realize people could have "we" time and also "me" time. For him, being connected to a woman in a meaningful relationship meant being tied down. And when he felt tied down, he suddenly would "fall out of love."

One time, however, I had a chance to catch him before another breakup.

"So, why do you think you want out of this relationship?" I asked. "Last time I talked to you, you felt like she was the one."

"I thought so," he lamented. "I really did. She is so awesome. But then she started to get controlling."

"Controlling?" I questioned.

"Yes. Like I wanted to go on a weekend trip with my buddies to go fishing, and she said she was sad because she wanted us to do something this weekend," he said.

"So, did she say you couldn't go? Or turn on the drama because you wanted to go away?" I asked.

"Not so much" he answered. "She was just saying she was sad, and I know what that means. It always happens. When I want to do my thing, they always begin to act like I am devastating them by not being with them all the time. I know what's next—all of the guilt and 'I thought you cared' stuff. And I just don't want to be with that kind of controlling woman," he continued. "I can't stand that kind of control."

"I'm not hearing any kind of 'control,'" I answered back. "I just hear someone who is saying she is bummed because you'll be gone, and she'll miss you. It sounds kind of appropriate to me, kind of sweet . . . unless she tried to keep you from going or something. Why does her being sad and missing you make her 'controlling'?"

"Because it is controlling," he pushed back. "Women just say they're sad so you'll feel bad and not go. She might as well just boil the bunny and throw a fit. It's all the same. I like her, but I have to have some space too."

"Are you *that* fearful?" I asked. "Are you so much of a child that you can't just say, 'Sorry this feels crummy. I get that. But we'll be together the next weekend' and just go and enjoy your trip? You are only controlled to the degree that you allow yourself to be. And I think a lot of your feeling controlled is in your head."

I continued, "Why don't you say to her, 'I need to understand something. Are you saying you don't ever want me to have any friends and spend any time away from you? Because when I said I was going away, you were sad, and that's how it seemed to me. So, is that what you meant?'"

I went on to say, "I think that might be better than throwing away another good relationship because you can't trust that someone is not trying to control you. Why don't you check it out and find out how much she really *understands your need for some freedom, and wants that for you?*" (Notice here the two essentials of trust: understanding him and having a motive for his good.)

We began to battle over this recommendation, and it slowly emerged that he even felt controlled by me giving this suggestion, feeling as though I was trying to force him to stay in the relationship. This was a great opportunity to hash it out with him and show him how vulnerable his "sunburn" was. It made him feel that anyone who wanted anything from him was trying to control him and take away his choices.

Fortunately, we were able to get to a breakthrough as he began to see that he was a grown adult and could say "no" anytime he wanted—to me or to a girlfriend. He found his freedom, if you will, which he'd always had but had not been internally free to use. Because he felt controlled by the voices inside of him, he heard every outside voice as one that was trying to turn him into a prisoner.

The inside voices that controlled him said, "Here we go again." But these feelings were coming from his past. During his formative years, his family, particularly his mother, used guilt messages to control him in many ways. When he wanted to make his own choices and not do what his parents wanted him to do, they piled on the guilt. "Okay, fine," they said. "Go be with your friends instead of with us. But it would seem that, after all we do for you, you could spend a little more time at home." Or, "You know how important baseball is to your father. How could you quit the baseball team to join the golf team? You know how much he loves you. How could you break his heart like this?"

His fear of being controlled had tied his trust muscle in knots. His freedom had never been established very well at the factory, and every time he got truly connected in a relationship that formed a "unit," as a real couple does (similar to a family), his internal voices told him he was no longer free and would either be subject to someone else's wishes or suffer the guilt of choosing things for himself. *You can't have both*, he heard in his head. So, we had some work to do.

Gradually he began to strengthen his ability to choose without guilt and he worked through the dynamic of turning every person he encountered into a controlling mother. He began to have good discussions when he felt controlled and he developed the capacity to stay in the conversation while asserting his freedom and wishes. He also gained the ability to compromise without feeling captured and held against his will. As he did these things, something amazing happened. He began to see a woman's request for him to spend time with her as an expression of love instead of a noose around his neck. Within a year, he was smitten, free, and engaged. I checked in on him not long ago, and he is still happily married after many years. Trust muscle repaired.

The thing to see here is that the majority of those controlling women who couldn't be trusted to give him freedom, as he saw it, were perfectly normal women with whom he could have had a great relationship and even marriage. It wasn't *that they were untrustworthy to give him freedom. He* was the one with trust issues, and his trust issues centered around *control.*

When we find ourselves struggling to trust, the problem isn't always that the other person or entity is not trustworthy.

The point I want to drive home here is this: when we find ourselves struggling to trust, the problem isn't always that the other person or entity is not trustworthy. Sometimes the issue is in the person who has to do the trusting, and they need to do some repair work. Their trust muscle, which was built in the past, perhaps even early in life, needs some healing so they can invest trust in trustworthy individuals. Trust is a two-way street.

ELEVEN

BREAKING YOUR TRUST BARRIERS, PART 2

In addition to the fears we explored in the previous chapter, there are other barriers to trust. Because this is not a book on healing all that is psychologically broken in us, I won't go into as much depth about the fears in this chapter as I did in the previous one. I went more deeply into the first two simply to illustrate how the fear dynamic influences our ability to trust and how trustworthy people may be unable to gain the trust of people who have trust issues. It really is important for us to see how our issues might be getting in the way of our trusting someone. Let's look at other fears that can get in the way of trust.

Fears Around Imperfection, Shame, and "Badness"

Human beings are not perfect, and those who are comfortable embracing this reality do best in life. Realizing that neither they nor the person they trust will be perfect allows them to pick the best "imperfect" people they can. As I always tell people, "Don't look for the person who is perfect or has no issues. Look for the one whose issues don't make you crazy or interact poorly with your own issues."

Let's think again about the developmental years. Some people grow up feeling they had to be perfect and flawless in order to be loved or accepted. Others have felt this way in past relationships. For some, perfection pertained to physical appearance, for others it was related to academic performance. For some it was about athletic accomplishments, and for others it had to do with their social life. The list goes on. Perfectionistic or narcissistic parenting or teaching styles can absolutely ruin someone's ability to trust. Inside their heads, the message they send to others is, "If I get close to you, and you really know me or see who I am, or if I fail or make a mistake, you will reject me, or you will not love me, or you'll shame me."

Perfectionistic or narcissistic parenting or teaching styles can absolutely ruin someone's ability to trust.

I recently worked with an executive team on which one member totally destroyed trust among the team's seven members. Every time she submitted an idea and the other team members didn't totally love it, she accused the team of not valuing her, "gaslighting" her, creating a "toxic work environment," and other negative behaviors. The truth was that they did value her, but as to everything else, they did not wholeheartedly embrace or agree with her every idea.

But if her ideas were criticized in any way, she accused the team or the boss of being "untrustworthy." Had she only been able to trust that they wanted her to be a part of the team and to contribute, things would have gone well. But she could not view them as trustworthy if they challenged or disagreed with her ideas, or were not thoroughly enamored of them. Her trust muscle demanded perfectly adoring responses to her at all times. Otherwise, she could not trust the team.

I did not know anything about this woman's past, as the project did not allow me to get to know her very well. But I can only imagine that it was one where she was either overly adored all the time and never had a chance to learn that she could be imperfect and still valued, or perhaps she was overly criticized and without acceptance, and she never learned that she could be imperfect, criticized, and valued all at the same time. Either way, her trust was still sunburned.

Narcissism is a big issue here. Narcissistic people have a great investment in being seen as "ideal" or "perfect." They must be adored and idealized by others in order to feel secure and trust. They cannot integrate the "good" and the "bad." They require others to see them as "all good." Then, similar to the woman in this story, when they are seen as not ideal, things do not go well and trust breaks down.

This becomes a difficult issue with men in marriage, as their brains get flooded with stress hormones much more quickly and thoroughly than women's brains.[*] As a result, when they are "criticized," in their minds, they are being "attacked." So trust goes out the window. For example, when a wife says to a husband, "Can you put your dirty dishes in the dishwasher?" and he hears, "You always criticize everything I do!" and gets flooded, trust gets broken. Trust is gone, but it is because his trust muscle is too broken to accommodate any negative input—even when it's not negative at all.

Similarly, narcissistic (and other personality disordered) people also often require others to be "all good" in order to trust them. They will idealize someone upon first meeting, fall in love with them (either romantically or in a business way), and think they have found the perfect "other," meaning romantic partner, company, boss, client, or church. They see this new acquaintance as "ideal." Finally, after the last loser they had, they have found the most awesome one ever.

When some sort of letdown or disappointment occurs, very quickly the new partner, company, boss, client, or church is "all bad." They have suddenly gone from being "wonderful" to "worst ever." This

---

[*] John M. Gottman, *The Science of Trust: Emotional Attunement for Couples* (New York: W. W. Norton & Company, 2011). Kindle edition.

is why trust is so difficult to build and sustain with people who have a great deal of narcissistic behavior. It is so unstable, so quickly interrupted by any perceived slight to the person's own ego or ideal image of themselves or their image of how the other person should be. This demand for perfection in the other person or institution can extend to demands for them to be flawless in every way. I have seen people suddenly jettison an entire relationship because of a few wrinkles, pounds, or a dip in a balance sheet. From good to bad, very quickly.

People who are comfortable with their imperfections are the ones who do well in trust. I was recently talking to a couple in their early twenties who had been dating successfully for two and a half years. I was impressed with their relationship and asked, "So what has made it go so well?" The young man said, "The thing I notice about our relationship compared to other people our age is that we both know we have flaws and we can own those in ourselves and each other. When they appear, we just talk about them and find a solution. It doesn't cause a big deal in our relationship." Not bad for twenty-one years old. I found myself not only wishing I had been like that at twenty-one, but also thinking that I know a lot of fifty-something-year-olds who would do well to be as mature as this young man. As he was talking about their being imperfect, she was nodding adoringly. It was a perfect picture: two imperfect people trusting each other!

Fears Around Trauma

"I don't know what's wrong," he said. "I love her. I know I do. But every time we get to a deeper place, I get so depressed and I just detach. I can't stand the feeling, so I have to end the relationship. I start to question her and just have to get out."

Another case of "getting close builds more trust, which leads to can't trust." But in this situation, it was not a fear of depending on someone, or control, or toxic perfectionism. His fear of trusting was caused by trauma.

This man had lost his mother at a young age, his caretaker "nanny" a few years later, and his stepmother when he was twelve. The counselor who worked with him right after his stepmother passed away died soon thereafter.

Needless to say, he had suffered much loss and his brain had learned something: attach to a woman, and you will lose her. Having never worked through his grief, each time he invested emotionally in a woman and began to love her, it tapped into all that loss sitting in his heart and soul.

Depression is often unresolved grief. So in the midst of what should have been a relationship moving in a positive direction, he would become severely depressed. His mind would say, "This is not the right woman or I wouldn't be so depressed." He would find a reason to question the relationship and get out of it. But actually, *the reason he felt depressed was that the woman was so good*! She was good enough to trust, which made him feel his heart, where the pain still lived. For him, to trust or to love meant to feel great pain and fear.

Other people have suffered abuse, abandonment, loss, multi-foster situations, molestation, and other awful traumatic experiences. On their own, these situations can stay adequately tucked away, compartmentalized in the basements of the human soul. But when people who have been traumatized get into a relationship that requires trust, trust does its job: it melts them and makes them vulnerable. That vulnerability exposes the sunburn to touch that is too much, and the trust goes away. It gets tested by acting out, the person begins to push the other away for little or no reason, and they abandon the relationship. People find all kinds of strategies designed to disrupt the enemy: trust.

Other trauma is simply about "the last time." I know and have worked with many people who are pretty well-developed, but really, really got burned in some adult relationship. As the saying goes, "A burned dog dreads the fire."

There is a phrase in psychology called "one trial learning." It basically means that while most learning is understood to take place through repetition, there are some instances where one experience is enough to damage a person's ability to trust for a long time. Some trauma is like that. A divorce, a breakup, a betrayal in a marriage or business—these are enough to tarnish someone's ability to trust deeply, after only a single, but awful experience. Getting left at the altar, being swindled by a business partner—situations such as these can destroy the ability to trust for a long time. Once someone learns how deep a hurt or betrayal can go, they avoid trusting. Just ask any victim of an affair how easily they are able to trust the person who comes into their life just after their ex. They will tell you that trauma can really get in the way of trust.

Fears Around Inequality

The discussion around feeling unequal often relates to diversity, as that dynamic can be so awful. I had a minority client who was very accomplished and smart. While no one would ever know how difficult it was for him to feel trust and to feel he was considered trustworthy, he suffered from it all the time. He confided in me that because he belonged to an ethnic minority group and had struggled against racism for most of his growing up years, trusting others in the business world was very difficult for him.

In the interactions I had witnessed, he was with totally trustworthy people who trusted him greatly. But because he had been hurt in the past, it was hard for him to overcome the fear of not being seen as an equal at the table. He was brilliant, and his colleagues viewed him as such, but his perception of always being seen as less-than-equal made it hard for him to trust that others actually saw him as they did. As he said, "When you are a minority, you have to outperform everyone else to be seen as equal to them." The truth was they already saw him as awesome.

Fortunately, with a lot of work, together with his team and his stakeholders, he was able to overcome his trust issues with them. He came by them honestly for sure, but they had left their scars. It took work on both sides for him to be healed, as it usually does. But he did it, and the trauma of feeling unequal to those around him diminished to a memory. It was beautiful to see him reach the point of being able to view himself as amazing as his teammates knew him to be.

But fears of not being seen as equal are not only about diversity issues. Some people are subject to the "one-down" dynamic because of developmental issues with domineering or critical parents, overly authoritarian parents, or even siblings or peers who acted superior to them. No matter how smart or accomplished these people are, they still feel beneath other people or are afraid they will be seen and judged to be so.

When someone doesn't respond to an email from them or include them in a thread, they feel marginalized. They can't trust the peer or team or person who left them out because they think people view them as inferior in some way. These feelings of "You never think I'm good enough"—or "whatever" enough—become barriers to trust.

A peer who struggles with being able to feel like a peer can have awful experiences in trusting others. Feeling one-down keeps them from speaking up, commanding respect, or feeling that their opinions are taken seriously. Before they say a word, they are sitting there thinking that their thoughts, skills, talents, or input will be viewed as inferior to other people's. It's hard to be "careless" when you feel that way, so trust diminishes.

In a twist for some people who feel inferior to others, they learned early: "If you can't beat 'em, beat 'em." Meaning they vowed early on when being put down or seen inferior, the best defense to that was to make themselves superior to everyone else. They solve the one-down dynamic by jockeying to be one-up. Everything becomes a competition for them, and they are determined always to be "right" or "better" than everyone else. They cannot trust equals because in their experience, and in their heads, there is no such thing.

A team I worked with recently had this issue with a new team member.

Alyssa had just finished the projections for the new project and wanted the boss, Nick, to see them. "I'll take it to him," Samantha said. "I'm headed up there anyway."

"But there are some line items that need explaining. I was going to let him know why we did it the way we did," Alyssa responded a bit quizzically. But she wasn't wondering about the line items. She was trying to figure out why Sam felt it so important that *she* take the report to Nick.

But, it did feel a little like . . . well . . . like the way Sam was. Sam seemed to be constantly working an angle with Nick, trying to put herself closer to him than Alyssa or others on the team. Alyssa didn't get why it had to be that way.

Before Sam joined the team, the dynamics were different. The group was more collegial, more collaborative. Now, there seemed to always be some sort of political angle going on—and more and more weirdness. She couldn't figure out why; she just knew that it had something to do with Sam.

When she told me about the interaction with Sam, and I asked her for some more examples, a pattern became clear. It wasn't about Alyssa, or any of the other team members. It was about Sam.

Alyssa shared: "She always has to have the last word, no matter what the team is discussing. And any time Nick is involved, she seems to put herself in the middle of whatever is going on just so she can be involved. And if she isn't, she questions why she wasn't included. If she's not included, she thinks it's for some nefarious reason. Then she almost throws the work into a different direction, where she is in control."

When I talked to other team members, they made comments such as, "She won't leave us alone to do our work. She has to be involved and somehow get a 'piece' of it in some way. She can't just trust us to do our part." And, "She has to come out seeming important—actually *more* important than anyone else. And she puts down other team members. That's the worst."

As the interviews continued, I could see that Sam was destroying the trust of a team of trustworthy people, *because of her own inability to trust.* It was becoming clear that to Samantha there was no such thing as a "peer" or an "equal." To her, everything was about someone either being one up or one down. Everything was a competition. Someone was going to win and someone was going to lose. And she was determined to always win, while making sure others lost.

Her competitive mentality made her afraid that if she didn't win, others would try to win over her. Her own competitiveness got in the way of trusting others, and made their trusting her impossible.

The fear that comes from seeing the world as an unequal place destroys a lot of trust.

The fear that comes from seeing the world as an unequal place destroys a lot of trust. Remember, trust is about being "careless," and when you fear that someone is always trying to defeat you, carelessness is hard. Competitiveness and divisiveness run rampant.

From sibling rivalry in families, which can go on for decades, to work teams, to circles of friends, the drive to be "better than," or "smarter than," or "liked and loved more than," or any other "more than" dynamic is a trust destroyer. People who have that dynamic in their own souls are afraid to let go and trust others who are completely trustworthy. They can't trust people they feel will try to best them in some way. So, instead of trusting, they compete and jockey for position. The trust issue is with them, not with other people.

These people have usually learned in their past that there are no real equals who can be trusted. Perhaps love or approval was given to a winner among siblings, or a parent competed with a child to never let them be equal to them, or one narcissistic sibling had to always be better than the others, or a love interest left them for someone else. For whatever reason, the person is now unable to view the world as trustworthy. They're convinced someone will try to do them in, and they are not going to allow that to happen. They're unhappy and so are the people around them. The consequences of a lack of trust.

Fears Around Oneself

I worked with one CEO couple in which the husband was extremely jealous. If the wife talked to a man at a party or had to work closely with a male client, he questioned everything. Seeing any of her relationships with other men as purely platonic was virtually impossible for him. He was constantly ripping their trust apart. And, the fact was, she was totally innocent and trustworthy.

But he wasn't.

In his past, he'd had numerous affairs. Not long after marrying his current wife, he was back at it. His trust issue was that he had never owned and overcome his own behavior. In simple psychological terms, he projected, meaning that he saw and feared in others behavior that was actually part of himself. He could not trust himself, so he could not trust his wife either.

I have also seen the same dynamic with overly rigid, especially religious types, who are constantly suspecting and jealous of their spouses, unable to trust, thinking that their spouse is either cheating on them or going to. But they themselves are very, very "moral."

Later, that same overly rigid moralistic person shows what all the rigidity was about; it was to keep themselves in check. This impulsive part of themselves was locked up in a cage or rigid moral structures. Very different from true morality, the judgmental type is rigid as an attempt at self-control. But when it finally cracks, you often see what was underneath the whole time.

Romans 2:1 says, "You, therefore, have no excuse, you who pass judgment on someone else, for at whatever point you judge another, you are condemning yourself, because you who pass judgment do the same things" (NIV).

Every judgmental person doesn't judge because they are like those they judge, but many are. Trust is almost impossible with a judgmental projecting person, because there is always something to be overcome—most of it imaginary.

This happens often with parents of teenagers. They try to control the you-know-what out of their teenage daughters (usually, it seems) because they remember what they were like as teenagers. If these parents were particularly promiscuous or acted out in some way, such as lying to their parents or experimenting with drugs, they will almost go crazy at times with imaginary scenarios involving their teens. So, they don't trust them. This *lack of trust destroys the relationship and actually creates what they fear.* The teen thinks, *Well, they aren't going to trust me anyway, even if I am good, so forget it. I'll do what I want.* Parents do well to know that trust breeds trust (remember the wife who trusted her husband when he had to take a business trip with his ex). But if they see their teenager as who they were thirty years earlier, instead of seeing the teen for who that young person is today, it becomes very difficult.

Seeing Old People in New People

In this chapter and the previous one, we've looked at various fears that create barriers to trust. The ones I've mentioned are not exhaustive;

there are more, but I wanted to focus on the most common ones. As we close this part of the book and prepare to move on, I'd like to call your attention to one more dynamic that can block trust. It's not a fear, but it is a problem we need to be aware of and overcome, if we find ourselves doing it. Think about this scenario:

A man moves to a new town. The first day he's there, he strikes up a conversation with the old man working at the gas station. He asks, "What are people like around here?"

The old man looks at him and replies, "What were they like the last place you lived?"

"Oh, they were pretty nice," he says.

"Well, that's probably how you'll find them here," says the wise old sage.

The man pumping gas knew that the new person in town's view of people would have as much to do with himself as the people themselves. Whatever he thought about his old community, he'll think about his new community.

Psychobabble or no psychobabble, we are products of our past. It's not that we have to be stuck in the past or never get over it. But until we do get over the past, it affects us. The axle is still bent, until it isn't. That's just true. People who have had bad experiences with authority figures, for example, often have skeptical views of authority, until that view is addressed.

If we can't see new people for who they are, our ability to assess them accurately will be impaired, as our own issues get in the way. As Jesus said, "First take the log out of your own eye, and then you will see clearly to take out the speck that is in your brother's eye" (Luke 6:42 ESV). Until we work out our own issues, we can't know others as they really are. We can't even see them. Maybe the new people aren't like the old ones at all.

We are well-served to always look at ourselves first. When we struggle to trust, the issue may not be that the other party is untrustworthy. It may be that we are unable to trust for some reason. Maybe our trust muscle needs a little repair work.

Embracing our issues and finding the healing we need is the first step of growth, and it's vital to building trust. The point of this chapter and the previous one can be summarized in this way: to make healthy and good decisions as to whom we will trust, we need to have healthy "trust equipment." So, work on yourself as well as evaluating others.

Growing in your ability to trust and developing a strong trust muscle will serve you well for the rest of your life. You'll be better equipped to make good choices about whom to trust. But as you may know from personal experience, no one makes perfect choices all the time. Again, trust is a two-way street. Sometimes trust gets demolished—and sometimes that experience comes as a complete surprise. At that point, it's necessary to have a path that will help you decide whether you want to trust again, whether the other person can be trustworthy, and how to repair broken trust. That's what the next section of the book is about.

SECTION 4

THE MODEL FOR REPAIRING TRUST

TWELVE

IT'S A PROCESS

Bella was dumbfounded. As she put it to me, through angry sobbing, "I just am without words. I can't believe he would do this. I can't believe it!" This was almost all she could utter. Over and over, she said, "I can't believe it. I never thought he could do this."

I couldn't believe it either, nor could many other people. Bella's husband, Drew, had been living a double life. He was a pillar of the community, a member of strong circles of friends and associates, someone she saw as a man of high morals and convictions and a committed Christian.

But the ugly truth was that he had been involved in a long-term affair with a colleague in his law firm for the past five years. And Bella had no idea. The situation was even more shocking because she knew the woman well. The firm did a lot of legal work for Bella's business and she was acquainted with her both professionally and personally. Their families had even spent time together. She was stunned.

To add insult to injury, it was through their family connection that the affair was discovered. Her son went to the other family's house to see if one of their college-age children was home, and he saw his dad's car parked there in the middle of the day. From there, you can guess what happened.

A great deal of chaos ensued. The partners at the firm were not happy with Drew, to say the least, and the woman ended up leaving the firm. Plus, Drew's fellow attorneys discovered that the current affair had not been his only screwup. There were other incidents as well.

Bella immediately separated from Drew. Their children remained with her and wanted nothing to do with their father. Bella was a wreck emotionally, simply trying to get through each day.

Eventually, through the support of a strong community of friends and church members and the help of some good professionals, things were stabilized for Bella. She was processing it all, trying to figure out whether or not she even wanted to think about staying together and working it out with Drew, as he begged her to do.

Broken, contrite, and *repentant* were words she used to describe how Drew was communicating to her, along with pleas to keep their family together and rebuild. She said to me, "I hate the thought of losing our family, but I have no idea how I could ever trust him again. I don't know how that works. And I don't know if I even want to try to find out. I just feel hatred for him more than anything, at least right now. How would I ever trust him again? How would I ever believe anything he says? I gave him everything. I can't do that again."

I totally understood. Given Drew's incredible capacity for duplicity and deception, I could see why Bella said, "I would need a crystal ball to be able to see the future before I could ever decide to give him another chance."

Bella was voicing *the* big dilemma:

After you have trusted, is it possible to trust again, and if so, how do you know?

Trusting again, once trust has been broken, is more than a decision. It is a *dilemma—a choice between equally unfavorable options.* If Bella doesn't trust again, she loses everything good about her relationship with Drew and their family. If she does trust him again, she feels she must deny the reality she has lived through. The thought of trusting Drew again makes her feel she would be putting her heart deliberately in the hands of someone who will hurt her. She was wrong to trust him once, she tells herself. She could be wrong again. In spite of the fact that Drew keeps promising to change, how could she ever know?

Trusting again, once trust has been broken, is more than a decision. It is a dilemma—a choice between equally unfavorable options.

Trust Doesn't Always Work Out the Way We Want It To

When we extend trust, sometimes we get duped. We can be fooled by someone who was so good at their duplicity that we could not have seen it. We truly are an innocent victim. And as all victims know, they didn't do anything to cause the problem the first time it happened, so it is possible it could happen again. Once again, they tell themselves, it would be completely beyond their control. They realize that because the person who hurt them so convinced them of his or her trustworthiness once, if they trust again, they could be fooled again. And then they would suffer the same consequences.

Sometimes, there were signs that someone wasn't trustworthy. Hopefully by now in this book, you are getting some new ways to spot some of those signs. And as we grow and learn, most of us can remember some situations where, as we look back, we can now see the signs that we didn't know to recognize then.

At other times, regrettably, people have a sense that someone isn't trustworthy, and for some reason, they trust them anyway. We'll cover some of the reasons for this in the last two chapters of the book, where we'll explore various reasons we trust people when we shouldn't. Situations such as these are so difficult because we keep telling ourselves, "I should have . . ." Then trusting becomes confusing again, because the same dynamics or weaknesses that made us ignore or minimize issues the last time are still present. That's a setup for a mistake to repeat itself.

And then, there's the biggest problem of all—trusting someone because he or she brought some really good things into your life, things you liked or even loved. You had good reasons for wanting to be aligned with this boyfriend or girlfriend, this business partner, this deal, this church, or this company. You saw tangible value and experienced many benefits as a result of this alliance. And now, if you only could trust again, you could have it all back—all the good. In many instances the reason you wish you could trust again is simply that you love this person or company or organization. You want the relationship and there are good reasons to want it. The thought of losing it hangs heavy.

But the dilemma remains. "To have all of that good back again," you tell yourself, "I must somehow get over this trust hurdle." It feels like jumping across the Grand Canyon flat-footed. You wonder, "How can I ever get over the belief and/or fear that betrayal will happen again?"

Good question.

As Bella said, you'd need a crystal ball. While I can't give you one of those, the goal of this section of the book is to give you the closest version of a crystal ball as I know: a way to evaluate if trusting again is smart.

As I have worked with people facing the dilemma of whether they should trust again or not, I've seen that one of the toughest issues they face is feeling they have to somehow read the tea leaves and discern whether or not the other person will be trustworthy. They watch every little ambiguous behavior or event. They become hypervigilant, looking between the lines, wondering how to interpret everything in order to make sure they don't get fooled again. The reality is that no one can do that. You can't be clairvoyant. So, unless you have that ability, you need another method. You can't ask yourself to be that kind of judge, seeing what is not visible. It will drive you crazy.

What you can do, however, is to look for some specific, objective factors. When these are present, the person or group of people in question are more likely to be worthy of someone you want to repair trust with than if the behaviors were not present. Instead of squinting to see between the lines in a situation with someone who has already hurt you once, you will know some obvious and specific actions to look for to help determine if the changes are going to be real or not, in addition to the five essentials of trust we've already discussed.

This way, trusting again is not a blind leap of faith, executed "in spite of" what the person has done to you. Instead, it is a choice you make *because* of certain, specific, objective behaviors you see. No crystal balls, no mind reading. Just clear observation, along with paying attention to your gut, soul, and internal realities.

The Steps to Repairing Broken Trust

The process of repairing broken trust is not one of blindly, and stupidly, trusting a betrayer again with a leap of faith that says, "It was horrible, but I love this person [or need this person) so much, and they are truly sorry, so I am going to forgive and give them another chance." **Instead, it is open-eyed, informed trust based on good, objective criteria. You need solid reasons to trust again.** *You will only trust because of certain factors that must be present before you extend trust again.* Hopefully, in this section of the book, you can get to a "go point," where you know you have reasonably good reasons to risk trusting again—or not.

In my experience, the question of restoring trust is about more than looking at whether this person is doing what they did before. The question is: "*Is this person pursuing a path that will make them someone who will not do what they did before?*" You need to know whether you are dealing with the same person—or a new one.

Equipping yourself to make that determination is a process that unfolds as you follow the six-step model for repairing broken trust:

Step 1: Heal from what happened to you
Step 2: Move beyond anger and revenge and turn toward forgiveness
Step 3: Ponder what you really want
Step 4: Figure out if reconciliation is available
Step 5: Assess trustworthiness
Step 6: Look for evidence of real change

Steps one through four will help prepare and equip you to see if trusting again is a possibility. They won't take you all the way to rebuilding trust after it's been damaged or destroyed, but they will help you know if you want to rebuild it and to decide if you and the other person can move in that direction. If you decide you are willing and ready to trust again, and that the other person is too, then steps five and six will move you toward that eventual reality, as they will teach you what to do and how to do it as you begin the delicate and important work of repairing broken trust.

While I've listed the steps of the model to rebuild broken trust in a linear fashion, repairing trust is not clean and orderly. You will cycle back and forth through these in a messy process. At the same time, to some degree, it is important not to skip steps.

In this section of the book, you may notice that some chapters, such as this one, are a bit short. This allows me to devote an entire chapter to each step of the process, and it gives you a chance to deeply process each one. This is heavy stuff. It can change your life in profound ways. So take your time as you go through each step.

Stop and think along the way. Highlight or underline. Journal. Pray or meditate. Talk about what you're learning with a trusted friend, counselor, coach, or therapist. Read and reread. Take time to process what you've learned in each step of the model before you move to the next one.

THIRTEEN

STEP 1: HEAL FROM WHAT HAPPENED TO YOU

The first step toward preparing and equipping yourself to repair broken trust in a relationship is all about you, not about the person who betrayed you. What must happen before anything else is healing—healing in your heart from whatever happened to break your trust in a person, a group, or an organization. It's about reaching the point where you are ready—emotionally and cognitively—to think about trusting again. There's no way for me to predict how long this healing will take or what all it will involve. Your situation is unique; your pain is individual. Your healing will take as long as it takes (and I encourage you not to try to rush it), and it will involve whatever is necessary to bring the relief, restoration, and wholeness your heart, mind, and soul need.

First, Take Time to Get Well

One of my favorite Bible verses says: "And make straight paths for your feet, so that *the limb* which is impaired may not be dislocated, but rather be healed" (Heb. 12:13 NASB). Other versions render the portion of the verse that pertains to "the limb which is impaired" this way: "so that it may not be put out of joint" or "disabled" (ESV; NIV). The idea is that when we are injured, we have to get well before we are ready to negotiate rocky paths in our current injured state, which might injure us more.

After my knee replacement, during the early weeks of physical therapy, the goal was to get the knee to flex to greater and greater measures. Every degree of movement you earn, you pay for with intense pain in physical therapy. The process is slow and excruciating. Each time you bend the new knee farther than you've bent it before, you think you might die of agony. In addition, you have to be very careful in your walking, choosing "straight paths for your feet" or you will pay for it. I was so careful with every step I took in order to avoid excruciating pain if I fell or moved my new joint too far, and to avoid damaging it as it healed.

One day a few weeks after surgery, in my early and fragile stages of walking, I took our Doberman pinscher, Finley, outside to use the bathroom. She was still in the training months, and I had her on a long training leash. We were walking toward one end of the pool when she saw a squirrel on the other side. You can envision what happened next. She instantly lunged toward the squirrel and raced around the end of the pool. I was not paying attention, and when she rounded the corner, the leash snapped taught, and pulled me into the water (she's a big dog). I was totally shocked, not even realizing what was happening. I certainly didn't have time to address my fall into the pool. I just was jerked into the shallow end, and I went in feet first with my surgical leg leading the way. I landed on that foot at the bottom of the pool, which was only a few feet deep. Needless to say, my leg did not hold and I went down on that leg, with the knee bending way past what I was able to bend at that point in my recovery. The pain was searing. I was in shock and almost began to lose consciousness as I lost my bearings.

Fortunately, I found the edge of the pool and was able to grip it. But the pain was indescribable. It was the kind of movement that should only be done under general anesthesia. Getting my bearings back, climbing out of the pool, and walking ever-so-gingerly back into the house took a while.

I was scheduled to see my physical therapist that day and was able to make it to the appointment. She looked at me and knew the situation was not good. Then she examined my knee. While she was sure I had not pulled out the implant (good news: I think they are very hard to rip out), my knee was very, very swollen and stiff. It was pretty much immovable. And it took a while for the swelling to go down and for me to get back to the point where I had been before the Finley incident. I had set myself back significantly.

Don't Set Yourself Up for a Setback

This is what Hebrews 12:13 is saying, and the story about Finley, the squirrel, and me in the pool illustrates the point of this chapter. When you are injured, you have to be taken out of the game until you get well, or the injured knee (or heart or mind) will get further damaged. You'll be set back in your healing and abilities if you get hit again. This is why, in the Superbowl, it is so devastating when someone gets injured. So much is on the line in that one championship game that a player may want to go to the sideline for a moment and quickly return to the game, despite severe pain. But the risk of ending a career prematurely or permanently damaging their body is not worth getting back into the game too soon. The player must remain on the sidelines until the medical team decides he is ready to play again.

When you are betrayed, you need time and healing.

When you are betrayed, you need time and healing. One of the main reasons you need these is that you can't even think well when you are significantly wounded. You will make bad choices. When you're in pain, the urge to withdraw, strike back, or make rash decisions is strong, especially if the betrayal is personal. The more your heart is involved, the greater the pain.

When betrayals are not personal, but professional, there is still wounding. In addition, security fears and anxieties kick in. A significant professional betrayal taps into many aspects of one's personhood. It may affect a current job or future employment opportunities, it may impact income and finances, or it may create other business or work-related anxieties. I have seen professional betrayals devastate people as much as marriage or other betrayals, especially when they take place between friends or family members.

When a betrayal happens in a business setting, people can be easily tempted to rush past it without taking time to heal. They may do this because they tell themselves, or others tell them, that business can be ruthless and they need to toughen up. They may also do it because money has been stolen in the midst or an income stream has been taken away because of the betrayal. Financial pressure is a strong motivator to get back to work without taking time to heal from a painful situation.

Regardless of whether trust has been broken in a personal relationship or a professional situation, when pain is present, healing is needed. Taking time to heal isn't just a good idea. It's necessary if you want to be able to trust again or to move forward in any area of your life.

Remember, "make level paths for your feet," as Hebrews 12:13 says (NIV). Whether personal or professional, the first step toward healing is always this: **connect with people you feel safe with and supported by, and let them help.** Don't isolate or withdraw or think you can be strong enough to heal by yourself. Even Navy SEALs need their buddies in times of battle. The people you connect with may be close friends, a therapist, a couples' counselor, a mentor, or a prayer group. If the betrayal is professional, you may also connect with a board of directors or lead investors in a business, trusted advisers, or your team at work (if appropriate). Other people bring valuable resources to your situation, resources that can help you get stable and healed. You need them to support and care for you, and you need their wisdom and the ability to help you figure out next steps. Support and wisdom are vital.

Allowing people to support you, care for you, and share their wisdom as you heal helps move you beyond the initial shock, numbness, denial, and catastrophic thinking that interferes with judgment, so you can process the pain. Even in a business setting, these emotions and thinking issues run rampant. I have seen high-level business leaders sustain betrayals by significant trusted parties and walk the same path emotionally as a jilted spouse or lover. Trust is a bond, an attachment, and no matter whether a breach of trust happens in a personal relationship or a business context, it can strike the heart the same way. So, the pain and wound require processing and time to bleed off the emotions. This will help you become strong enough to move into the next step.

What Happens When People Don't Heal

When people don't take time to heal, several bad moves can be made. For example, in a nonobjective or defensive state of woundedness, they can make horrible decisions and mistakes. Or they can get taken advantage of in significant ways because they are so vulnerable and just looking for a way forward.

How many times have we heard of a husband who betrays his wife and then says, "You don't need an attorney. Of course, I'll take care of you and the kids." Not only will he many times not take care of anyone but himself, she needs the protection of someone in her corner, and it certainly should not be him. But in a state of shock, hurt, and confusion, the betrayed one is very vulnerable and needs help to even know where to turn next.

When you are injured, you are often not going to do your best thinking. There's no shame in that. It's just a fact. And, many times, you have never even been in this scenario before and you have no idea how to think about what is happening in the moment or what needs to happen in the future. You need healing, and you need strong advisers to help you operate from a stronger place.

FOURTEEN

STEP 2: MOVE BEYOND ANGER AND REVENGE AND TURN TOWARD FORGIVENESS

"**A**re you kidding me? I can never forgive that x*&#$ for what he did!" If you are anything like Bella, and if you have been betrayed significantly enough, you can probably relate to at least feeling this way. Forgiveness feels so impossible at times, so unfair, and even wrong. But here is the best truth I can share with you about it:

If you are going to be your best, healthiest, and highest performing self, you must forgive.

Forgiveness is the way you free yourself from betrayal. Otherwise, you'll be tied to it and trapped in it for the rest of your life. Forgiveness certainly is a gift you give "to" someone who has hurt us. When we give it, we enable them not to punish themselves for their wrongdoing and sometimes (as we shall see) open the possibility of a future relationship unstained by past failure. But forgiveness is also a gift you give yourself, and I want you to see the value it has for *you*. To hold on to an injury and to nurse anger and bitterness, is to allow a cancer to grow in your heart, mind, and soul. It will kill you, physically and otherwise. Here are some overwhelming facts from scientific research about how forgiveness affects us. Forgiveness:

- Improves mental health
- Decreases rumination
- Reduces or eliminates painful and damaging emotions, such as resentment, bitterness, hatred, hostility, residual toxic anger, revenge wishes and motivation
- Reduces depression
- Reduces anxiety
- Aids in addiction recovery
- Helps the PTSD healing process
- Reduces chronic stress
- Improves mortality rates
- Lowers blood pressure
- Lowers cholesterol
- Resolves ongoing relationship struggles and chronic interpersonal disturbances
- Increases immune system functioning
- Decreases heart disease
- Increases agreeableness and lowers neuroticism
- Breaks the link between chronic stress and poor mental heath
- Reduces pain
- Increases the ability to judge people accurately

As researcher Dr. Loren Toussaint says, "Forgiveness is a topic that's psychological, social and biological." He adds, "It's the true mind-body connection." Forgiving people when they have hurt you, betrayed you, or otherwise wronged you is very important for your whole system. When you carry around unforgiveness, your mind, body, and soul produce toxic, fight or flight, cancerous emotions, chemistry, thoughts, and behaviors. And when you forgive, the mind-body relationship begins to clean out, clear up, and heal.

Forgiveness is the way you free yourself from betrayal.

This is why the people who really understand forgiveness work hard on it in their own lives. Take, for example, forgiveness researcher Dr. Bob Enright, a psychologist at the University of Wisconsin, Madison. A pioneer in forgiveness research who says that true forgiveness can take you to a stronger, virtuous place, he has earned the right to make bold claims about the power of forgiveness. He had to work through forgiving a man who murdered his mother in a home invasion. He knows how difficult and painful certain situations can be, yet how essential forgiveness is. He remains a strong proponent of forgiveness, even for horrible wrongs.[*]

Unforgiveness Isn't Worth the Damage It Does

Unforgiveness can turn you into a bitter, vengeful person. It causes you to lose aspects of your soul and life to the person who betrayed you. As long as you hold on to what wrong they did, they still own you. As I heard someone say once, "When you remain angry, you are just a character in someone else's story." When you let go and forgive, you are free to write your own story. You do not have to be worried about settling an old score.

---

[*] Kirsten Weir, "Forgiveness Can Improve Mental and Physical Health," *American Psychological Association*, January 2017, https://www.apa.org/monitor/2017/01/ce-corner.

I recall working with a woman whose husband had betrayed her. She was stuck in "I-will-punish-him" mode for quite a while. I so grieved when I saw how paralyzed she was, how obsessed she was with what he had done, and how difficult she found it to move on. She wouldn't work through her grief and unforgiveness. She was stuck in her anger.

One day she walked into my office with a look of glee on her face. I asked her what she was so smiley about, and she said, "His Mercedes was parked in the parking lot of this building and as I walked by it, I keyed it all the way down the side. He loves that car more than life. I hope he suffers."

I sank inside as I thought about how far she had to go on her healing journey and how miserably stuck she would be until she could release the anger and let him go. She was headed for a lot of misery until then.

The verdict is in. If you are going to be healthy, you have to forgive. Period.

I have seen people who were jilted in business take the same stance toward whoever betrayed their trust. One man whose business partner had betrayed him spent several years scheming and figuring out a way to ultimately conquer his foe by taking over the other man's business through a long-term strategy. It is so sad to have such a big part of one's life dictated by another person's actions. When people allow this to happen, it makes them a slave to those who hurt them in the truest sense, even if they "win." They never had their own life; the one who hurt them was in charge of it all along as the one who got hurt felt compelled to get even.

The verdict is in. If you are going to be healthy, you have to forgive. Period.

Feel the Anger and Express It Appropriately

I could write an entire book on forgiveness, but this book is about trust, and this section is about repairing trust. Forgiveness is a prerequisite for repair. Without it, trust will remain broken indefinitely.

Repairing trust involves coming to the table with a clean agenda to find the best future. If we are holding on to the desire to punish someone, it is difficult to work out a good tomorrow. Forgiveness is the way to deal with the past and get it out of the way so it does not ruin the future. We can't work out a relationship with someone we are punishing.

The problem is that forgiving someone isn't quick, clean, and easy. You will still have feelings that are real and must be acknowledged until they are gone. When you begin to work out a relationship with someone, anger and hurt will resurface—and I'll address that later in the book. It is naïve to think that forgiveness will be tidy and cause a painful situation to suddenly be "over." It's not like flipping a switch; it's a process.

But there is a big difference between anger and hurt that are expressed in the work of reconciliation, and anger and hurt that are expressed in a retaliatory way. One leads to healing and understanding in the relationship, while the other leads to further alienation. Forgiveness is putting down the sword to see what is possible for tomorrow. And it means giving up any sort of angry stance.

Resolving anger is one of the biggest aspects of forgiveness. It is essential to the process, in both directions: *you must have anger to get better, and at some point you must give up the anger to get better.* By "have anger" I mean that to forgive someone, you have to be honest about blaming them. They are guilty. Period. They did something harmful or painful to you. You cannot deny what they have done and expect to forgive them well. Forgiveness requires a wrong. So call the wrong what it is, and name it. Be honest about it. And know that doing so will lead to a period of anger. So, face the fact that you are angry about it. Of course you are. They did something really bad to you.

Anger is an emotion that says "something is wrong." It is a protest emotion, meaning that it gears up the system for action to fight something that is wrong. So, if there has been a betrayal, you are going to be angry about it. That is okay and good. The issue is how you handle your anger and what you do with it. It can be destructive, or it can be a force for good.

One of my favorite verses is Ephesians 4:26: Be angry, but "in your anger do not sin" (NIV). God designed the human system to emotionally protest injustice. Allow yourself to feel and express anger, but don't do anything destructive in the process. Don't act it out; talk it out. "Do not repay anyone evil for evil," as Romans 12:17 says (NIV). Don't hurt anyone in the process, just get the anger *out*, meaning, *get it out of your soul*. It has to be expressed and worked through. It needs to be "bled off."

**Anger is an emotion that says "something is
wrong." It is a protest emotion.**

Research has shown that continuous expressions of rage for a long time do not end the rage. It's not like you have a bucket of anger you need to keep dumping until it is empty. There is, however, a need to get in touch with the anger and express it, because doing so is an important part of validating what has happened to you. It can also motivate you to take steps to solve the issue and not get hurt again. Anger is important. It is an emotion that tells us something is wrong.

But to continuously fan it forever, feed it, and think that expressing it in an ongoing way is somehow going to help you is just wrong.

When people continually feed and vent their anger, their "stance" of being angry and their internal opposition to the person who hurt them becomes fixed, in a way. It becomes a part of "who they are." So, it just produces more anger. If ongoing expressions of anger were the resolution, then terrorists and lifelong hotheads would be the models of mental health. But, as we all know, that isn't the case (even though a lot of therapists haven't gotten the memo). Anger points us to a problem, then our reality and our values ask us to resolve it. We need to get past anger for our own good, and for the hope of anything good ever happening. As it is expressed adequately, and then healing of the wound happens and power is regained, the anger diminishes.

After You've Dealt with the Anger, Forgive

After dealing with your anger—or more accurately, as you deal with it over time—look at a different stance than the one that is producing anger: the stance of forgiveness. This means putting yourself in a different place than you were in relation to the person who betrayed you. In the forgiveness stance, you are no longer against them. The stance of forgiveness leads you to say, "I am going to cancel the debt that I have against you. You no longer owe me for what you did. I am letting you off the hook for what you did to me. I forgive you."

If this is hard to swallow because you feel it opens you up to being hurt again in the future, let me remind you:

Forgiveness has to do with the past. Trust has to do with the future.

Forgiveness cleans out the past so you can evaluate what you want to do with the future. Just because you forgive someone does not mean you trust them. Forgiveness is free. It's something you grant a person for no reason having anything to do with them. You do it for your own good, so you can move beyond the pain of what they did to you.

Trust, on the other hand, is not free at all. It must be earned and deserved. You do not have to trust people. If you do, it should only be because they have earned it, hopefully in the ways we will be looking at in later chapters of this book. But whether or not you go forward and have any kind of relationship with the person who hurt you, forgiveness is key to your future. And ultimately, if you want to repair the trust, it is absolutely essential.

Just because you forgive someone does not mean you trust them.

Forgiving People Who Don't Deserve It or Desire It

One note about forgiving someone who does not deserve it and may not even want it: something in all of us recoils at the idea of granting forgiveness to someone who doesn't seem interested in having it, nor has even tried to seek it. What has helped me understand this is the gospel. Whether you are a person of faith or not, I think the way the Bible describes God's forgiveness is a great model for us in terms of how to take this life-saving step. So even if you are not from a faith perspective, follow the story of the way the forgiveness process unfolds.

The Bible says that "while we were still sinners, Christ died for us" (Rom. 5:10 NIV). God freely gave forgiveness to the whole world through Jesus's death, and no one had even asked Him for it. No one had confessed that they had betrayed Him by rejecting Him and His ways. He simply forgave, on His own. That solved it all for Him. And he was done with the past, free from it.

Jesus said just as He died, "It is finished." In its original language, the word He used for *finished* actually means "paid in full, fully executed or discharged, or reached the end."* As the Bible explains, God had dealt with the anger, and fully canceled the debt. Forgiveness was given to all.

Now, as we said, it only takes one person to forgive. He did that. But it takes two people to reconcile (we'll look at this in detail in chapter 16). While He offers forgiveness to everyone, not everyone is reconciled in a relationship with Him. That kind of relationship requires something from them. They have to confess that they have sinned against Him, say they are sorry, and repent. If they do, then the relationship between Him and them is reconciled and restored. This doesn't mean that God will automatically trust someone with some big responsibility, job, or mission, just because He forgave them. Trust, as He says in many places, comes as a person is faithful with little before they can be trusted with more (Matt. 25:23).

So, the model of forgiveness presented in the New Testament is a good one for us: forgive no matter what the other person is doing so you can be "finished" with the transgression. If the person admits what they did and says they are sorry, then be reconciled. And you are back to a good place. From there, you can see whether or not they are able to earn your trust going forward, as we shall explore.

---

* James Strong, *The New Strong's Expanded Exhaustive Concordance of the Bible* (Nashville, TN: Thomas Nelson, 2010).

FIFTEEN

STEP 3: PONDER WHAT YOU REALLY WANT

"I never want to see that x*&#$ again," Greg said. "And if I do, I'm afraid of what I might do to him."

Greg had started a company, and a few years later, he entered into a relationship with another company whereby it got a minority, but significant, interest in his business. He did not like that his board and investors had wanted to do this deal, as he'd had prior dealings with the CEO of the other company, Rob, and did not trust him. His mistrust didn't come from experiences where Rob had lied, cheated, or lacked integrity, but from a general impression and some experiences that indicated Rob was always simply out for himself. He did live up to his commitments, thus making others *think* he was trustworthy. But Greg felt Rob could not be trusted to have your back if the contract didn't obligate him to do so. You could count on him to look out for himself, but he would not be worrying about what you needed.

Remember, part of our definition of betrayal is when one person acts in their own interests only, with no consideration for the other's well-being. But Greg's board trusted Rob and felt that as long as they made sure they had a tight contract that gave him little leeway in his legal obligations to the deal, everything would be okay.

This takes us back to one of the lessons we learned early in this book: trust involves more than one factor. An absence of lying or cheating is not sufficient to trust someone. We talked about the five essentials of trust, and Greg's fear was based on one of them: Rob's motives were 100 percent for himself. His entire intent was for his own interests, *not* the interest of Greg and his stakeholders. And that is exactly what occurred.

After gaining a large minority interest in Greg's company, Rob went behind Greg's back and made a huge financial offer to one of Greg's close friends and partners, someone Greg had started the company with. The partner sold his interest in the company to Rob, and suddenly, in what was a hostile takeover among "friends," Greg lost control of his baby to Rob. Before this move, Greg and his original partners, both friends, had control of the company with a combined ownership of more than 50 percent. But when one of them sold out to Rob, Rob seized control of the business Greg had started, his entire heart and passion.

Greg was devastated, wounded, scared of what would happen next with the business. Rob had a very different business philosophy than Greg. He was interested in profits above all else, while Greg was interested in the mission of the company and its people before profits. The two men were like oil and water. And what was so sad was that Greg *knew* he could not trust Rob before this happened. He did not want the deal in the first place. But his board and investors did, so it went forward. He felt like an idiot for allowing that to happen, but he had tried to be a good team player and do what everyone else wanted.

So, he found himself in a situation where he just wanted to either get out of the business altogether or sue them and inflict pain on Rob. Fight or flight was pretty much all he could feel. Get away or go after them. He was angry and devastated. And, as we learned in the chapter on healing what from happened to you when trust has been broken, in that state of mind, he could have made some dumb decisions.

Thankfully, Greg's board and his other partner had a cooler head. They were not nearly as wounded as he was, since it was his baby from the beginning. Nor had they been as close to the partner who sold him out as Greg was, and that was the deeper betrayal. They were thinking more strategically than he was. He wanted to sell out or blow it up. They asked a different question:

What is the best outcome we could imagine?

After a while, they brought in a consultant and a wise board member and went away to process. Thankfully, step one of the model of restoring broken trust—dealing with anger and turning toward forgiveness—had had enough time to do most of its work by this point. Greg had yelled, cried, stormed, ranted, and worked through the initial bleeding of his deep wound. He had reached the point where cooler heads had gotten him to begin asking "What do we really want?" He was not 100 percent there, but he was calm enough to proceed.

They began to weigh their options. No one liked that Rob had gained control of the company. No one had intended for that to happen, and after his behind-the-back trick to buy out the other partner, they all felt betrayed. What were they to do now?

They could all sell out to someone else, take their money off the table, and move on. Then they wouldn't have to deal with Rob. But this would also certainly come with noncompete issues and they would not be able to continue doing what they loved. Also, if they chose this option, the problem would certainly become public and reveal a serious parting of the ways. A big public fight would damage other people's trust in them and their brand as well, and they had solid, hard-earned reputations to protect. They knew that even when a party is completely innocent, someone finds a way to villainize them with an alternative narrative. They did not want a fight in the media or in the industry community. In addition, the company would sell at a multiple of revenues or profits, and they were just beginning to reach the tipping point where things would go upward very strongly. Now was not the time to sell, because a future multiple would be much bigger as earnings would come from the expansions they had invested in for the past few years. Selling out was not an attractive option.

They then began to consider finding a way to work with Rob going forward, and for good reasons. Even with the aspects that Greg didn't like about this possibility, the combined entity would certainly be stronger, offer more opportunities, and bring many other benefits. He would just have to swallow a lot of things that tasted pretty bad along the way. That wasn't tenable for him, so the question began to form, "How can we make this work and limit the aspects of it that I just can't 'swallow'?"

Ultimately, that's what they did. They figured out that the benefits of staying with the company and the new combined partner entity was the best option, if they could repair the relationship to some working fashion and limit the negatives. Through the process of restoring broken trust outlined in this book, they were able to do that, even though it took a lot of effort, work, time, and expense.

For the purpose of understanding this step of "figuring out what you want," we need to see that sometimes we really need to take some time and space to work through alternative scenarios. In the case of Greg's company, what would selling out mean? What would suing and going to battle mean? What would staying together and trying to work with Rob mean? How would all of the options affect the stakeholders? What are the different financial factors and how do they weigh in? There were many other considerations, and they were worth thinking about.

Should You Stay or Should You Go?

At some point, in some context, you may need to decide whether to stay in a situation and try to repair a relationship or whether you would be better served to move on:

- Do you divorce or try to stay together after a deep betrayal, once you consider the children, the benefits of the relationship, faith, love, and more? Is trust possible?

- Do you continue to work at a company you feel betrayed by once you consider the full impact your leaving could have on you and your family, or when you think about the effects staying might have on your heart, mind, and soul? Can the dilemma be worked out satisfactorily or not? Is moving on worth a total career overhaul?

- Do you remain in a church after the leadership has betrayed the membership, including you? Is the community you have there too strong to simply jettison, even if you can't agree with some leaders or what they did? Are children involved, and if so, how would their spiritual formation be affected?

- Do you try to repair a relationship with a close friend or extended family member after a significant betrayal? Who else is involved, and what other relationships are affected by your decision to stay or to move on?

There are many other factors to consider when you're trying to decide whether or not you want to try to trust again. Right now, you may not know what the best decision will be. A lot may depend on what the other person or party does and what they want. But at this point you can certainly begin to evaluate the situation and ponder:

- What would I like to see, given these circumstances?
- Are there good reasons to pursue rebuilding this relationship?

- Are there things worth fighting for?
- Are my eyes finally open and can I see that there is nothing here to keep me another day?
- Is there a "bigger picture" than just this person and what they did to me?

Do some deep soul searching to find what you really want. And remember: *This step is not to ponder whether or not you will forgive. You are going to do that, and you are going to offer the person the chance to apologize and receive that forgiveness.* This pondering is about "Now that I have dealt with what happened, what would I like to happen going forward?"

You can always say, "I forgive you," and "I wish you well," and have no desire for an ongoing relationship or to work with that person or organization. You may decide not to trust again. As Ecclesiastes 3:5 says, there is "a time to embrace and a time to refrain from embracing" (NIV). You forgive, but you do not want to go to another prom, or start another company with that person. You don't want to stay in the marriage or continue the level of relationship you had before the betrayal. Sometimes, after a betrayal and some deep soul searching, you realize your time with someone has ended, and you move on.

But, other times, there is much to save. There is much to be had in the future if things can get worked out. I have seen horrible betrayals healed and relationships turned around. I've witnessed couples enjoy their best decades of marriage *after* a betrayal, years that were better than their time together before trust was broken. Many times, this is because of the work that was done to repair the trust. It is possible, and it happens every day. You just have to figure out if you really want it.

One more thing. More often than not, pondering what you want is an unfolding process. Sometimes you can't know what you want until you have engaged in some of the steps we'll look at in later chapters because you don't really know if that person is changing or not. You don't yet know who you are dealing with—Jekyll, Hyde, or someone (hopefully) new. Don't feel you have to have it all figured out right now. But do begin the process of pondering what you really want so you will have a direction moving forward. I know what you *really* want is for the betrayal to never have happened! But this step involves letting go of that wish, seeing reality, and asking yourself, "Given where we are now, what do I want going forward?"

Once you've begun to ponder what's next, let's examine further what repairing trust looks like.

SIXTEEN

STEP 4: FIGURE OUT IF RECONCILIATION IS AVAILABLE

In the previous chapter, we acknowledged the dilemma of thinking about trusting someone again once they've failed you. It leaves you caught between two opposing drives—the desire to have the good things the relationship can bring us and the desire to not be hurt or damaged in some way again. The dilemma arises because both drives are valid. There are good things to want, and there is reason to be wary. So, what to do next?

We figure out if reconciliation is available.

This doesn't mean trust will be repaired. It's just the next step in that direction, and it will help you see who you are dealing with.

Reconciliation is returning a relationship to "good standing." It does not automatically include trusting the person going forward, although it may evolve to that. It is simply forgiveness on your part plus the other person apologizing and owning what they have done so you can return to a good, forgiven place, no matter what you decide to do in the future.

Before we go on, I'd like to give you some hope regarding a few people you already know. Remember our opening story about the CEO and the board chair? The chairman was walking out the door. It looked like their relationship was over. The ending? Trust was repaired and the CEO had a successful fifteen-year run after the scene I shared with you.

Remember Bella? Her husband, Drew, betrayed her with a double life and affair? Today, ten years later, they are having the best marriage they've ever had and have surpassed what they had always dreamed of. And his law firm is thriving.

And Greg from the previous chapter? Greg, Rob, and the rest of the team restored their relationship, and now, twenty years later, they work well together and are enjoying one another.

With these updates, I don't mean to imply that every broken trust story ends in victory. It doesn't. If you recall, Sean didn't make a breakthrough. That's how trust is. It always takes two parties to make it work. So, no guarantees.

But I can tell you that the plan for repairing trust works, if you work the plan. If two people or entities follow the model and engage in the process, it certainly can work. **But both have to engage** and be willing for it to work well. And obviously the untrustworthy behavior must have ended.

Determine Who You're Dealing With

Olivia had begun her home accessories company with a rocky start, but she soon realized that all she needed to get over the growth curve was to find the right business development person. She had a great furniture product line and was well-connected in her industry. But her focus was on design, branding, and manufacturing. She knew her business could go to the next level if she could find the right business development person who could grow the revenues.

When she found Derek, it seemed like a business marriage built in heaven. Derek was a get-it-done machine and loved knocking down barriers. They had so much energy and momentum. For a year or so, things were humming very well. There was a lot of excitement and big dreams for the future. With a few big sales to major retailers under their belt, it seemed like the sky was the limit.

One day, Olivia got a call from her accountant with some questions regarding strange charges on the corporate credit card. She pulled the statement up online and was puzzled by a few items from golf resorts and high-end sports and men's clothing retailers. These purchases didn't make sense to her, so she asked her bookkeeper to dig a little deeper. What she found was shocking. What occurred next, though, was devastating.

Derek had charged tens of thousands of dollars to the business card for personal expenses. Trips with his wife and her family, personal vacations, and retail purchases were all clearly right there. Discovering that Derek had been using company (Olivia's) money for himself without telling her was the shocking part, and it hit her hard. But she trusted him fully and thought, *I'm sure there's a good explanation for this. I'll just ask him about it.* When she did, however, his answers felt evasive and unsatisfactory. In fact, he seemed to be hiding something. That's when I was invited into the situation as a consultant.

Then the devastating part ensued. Olivia, two board members (who were also investors), and I met with Derek, and he completely denied any wrongdoing. He basically explained away everything, saying the purchases were gifts to contractors or clients, legitimate business expenses, or bonuses he paid himself for deals he personally negotiated instead of using the sales team. "I actually was saving the company money," he explained. Somehow, he thought making financial decisions to benefit himself and paying himself without sharing it with Olivia was okay. The board and investors were livid at this finding.

But there was a bigger problem. Olivia knew from additional fact discovery that many of Derek's explanations were absolutely not true. They were outright proven *lies*. And apart from the lies about expenses and money, she was finding that Derek had lied to her about other parts of the business he was responsible for as well. His comments about the situation reeked of duplicity and secrecy. She looked into it more and found he had abrogated many of his fiduciary responsibilities in the company and exposed her to a lot of liability. The board members were ready to take action.

Olivia, however, really wanted to find a way to continue working with Derek, hoping for the best to come out of it. She loved Derek; they were such close friends and confidants. But the board members forbade any ongoing working relationship. Their thinking was not clouded from the close personal bond that Olivia shared with Derek, having spent so much time in the trenches. For them, the issue was clear: Derek did not take responsibility for doing anything wrong, nor was he remorseful for how he had hurt Olivia and the investors. Instead, he justified it and said he had nothing to apologize for.

That, for them, was the clincher. They could have forgiven Derek and possibly figured out a way to try to go forward had he simply owned his actions and agreed that he had been wrong and what he had done was harmful. But in the end, he did not see that he had made any mistakes in playing loose with the finances, betraying trust, and taking money without their knowledge. And worse, they discovered that in his negligence, he had broken several laws, including some that created significant tax issues that cost the company a lot of money to rectify.

After several consults that determined Derek really could have gone to jail and after his continued refusal to admit his mistakes, the board members felt they had been seriously betrayed. Their trust had been abused, and they were very angry.

But Olivia was heartbroken. She wanted Derek to apologize, and she still wanted to trust him. She told herself his explanations were kind of believable—until she thought about the situation objectively. Then she had to face the truth. He never saw himself as wrong, never owned anything, and never apologized. Their working relationship was truly over.

Do They Take Real Responsibility?

Olivia's story helps us understand what we must do when figuring out whether reconciliation is available when a betrayal has occurred. We must determine who we're dealing with. We start this process by asking several questions:

1. Do they take responsibility for what they did?
2. Do they see how what they did was wrong?
3. Do they recognize the consequences of their behavior and understand how it has hurt you or others?
4. Are they remorseful, sorry, and contrite?
5. Do they repent and apologize for their actions?
6. Are they transparent with information, and do they give you full access to the truth?
7. Are they coming clean with the "whole story"?

If someone is fully honest, remorseful, and apologetic—and if they care about what they have done to you and desire to make it right—then your forgiveness can go to the next level: you can be *reconciled in the relationship.*

Notice that I did not say you can trust again. Not yet. All this step involves is "apology accepted" and "relations restored." You're letting the person know that you no longer hold the offense against them and that it no longer comes between the two of you. You can move toward feeling that the problem is in the past and move forward in whatever relationship you deem appropriate. This is the stance that many ex-spouses take with each other in co-parenting, for example.

This is usually all it takes to reach the point of reconciliation. Remember, *I'm not referring to trusting again. I'm only talking about reconciling the relationship to a good, forgiven place.* You may or may not be able to extend trust again. This depends on many other factors as we shall see. **Reconciliation is only the first step.** But with forgiveness from your side, and clear ownership and responsibility and remorse and repentance on the other side, you can at least return to a place where you are okay with each other.

You may decide at this point not to have an ongoing relationship with the person or you may decide to be friends with that person without trusting as you did before. You may even reach a place of full repair. *But no matter where you land with the other person, being okay with them requires ownership, apology, remorse, and repentance on their part. A heartfelt, "I'm sorry" goes a long way.*

The alternative to owning and sincerely apologizing for hurting someone is to say, "It's not my fault," in some way. This may take the form of various avoidance-of-responsibility defenses:

- Denial
- Lying
- Gaslighting
- Blame
- Excusing
- Minimizing
- Rationalization
- Invalidating
- Entitled to someone else taking responsibility for the problem
- Projection

Any of these behaviors make moving on difficult. The best option becomes, "We'll have to agree to disagree," which doesn't get you very far in the context of a true betrayal.

Psychiatry and psychology, and in some ways the legal system, distinguish between owning bad behavior and disowning it. The legal system may offer reduced sentences or no jail time and other leniencies if someone simply apologizes and truly shows remorse and repentance for their wrong. It puts that person in a different category than one who does not take responsibility.

Years ago, psychiatry and psychology developed a distinction between neurotic disorders and character disorders. Some used to joke that neurotics feel "over-responsible" and character disorders feel "under-responsible." There are some real accuracies to that distinction. "Neurotics" tend to feel guilty and anxious about things they *didn't* do, and people with "character disorders" don't feel bad or anxious about what they *did* do.

Interestingly, the Bible was way ahead of psychological research in this area, as it draws three conclusions about people, based on their behavior. You can read about these in detail in my book *Necessary Endings*. But for our purposes here, I simply want to point out how the Bible characterizes people when they are corrected and when they make mistakes, so you can keep it in mind as we continue learning how to repair trust. It describes them in three ways: wise, fools, and evil.

Wise People

The first group are the wise. Among other good qualities, a wise person possesses an essential personal trait that is apart from intelligence. It's the ability to be able to **listen** to a confrontation about his or her behavior, **own** it, **apologize**, **learn** from it, and **behave differently** as a result of being corrected. Proverbs 15:31 (NLT) says:

> *If you listen to constructive criticism, you will be at home among the wise.*

The Bible also says that instead of acting with defensive anger and turning against you, a wise person will actually be grateful to you for pointing out their mistakes or errors:

Correct the wise, and they will love you. —Proverbs 9:8 NLT

When dealing with wise people, the conversation feels open, soft-hearted, and "other-oriented." They *listen.* They don't excuse their behavior, blame it on someone else, or try to avoid consequences by deflecting responsibility. The conversation goes well and ends well. It involves listening, learning, caring, remorse, and change. Incredibly deep, moving moments can take place in interchanges when someone who messed up takes responsibility for hurting someone else and reconciliation occurs. This can only happen when dealing with a wise person. Unfortunately, everyone isn't wise. That's why the Bible also speaks of fools or mockers.

Fools or Mockers

The second group of behaviors is referred to as belonging to "fools" or "mockers." This refers to actions totally unlike those of the wise. Whereas wise people do well when confronted or corrected, fools or mockers will get defensive and engage in several problematic responses. Proverbs 9:8-9 (NIV) teaches:

Do not rebuke mockers or they will hate you;
rebuke the wise and they will love you. Instruct the
wise and they will be wiser still.

People who respond in foolish or mocking ways do **not come close to accepting responsibility** for what they have done or **how they have hurt you.** In fact, they either blame you or someone else for the problem. When confronted or corrected, they are **defensive** and **angry**, even **attacking**, as Proverbs 9:7 (NLT) tell us:

Anyone who rebukes a mocker will get an insult in return.
Anyone who corrects the wicked will get hurt.

Clearly, all people are not the same. There are those with whom you can have a redemptive, constructive conversation and those you can't. When you're thinking about repairing trust, it's crucial to know what kind of person that person is being at that juncture.

I would offer a caveat here to the category of "fool," and it applies to each of us. We can all be defensive at times. This often happens when certain buttons related to the areas of woundedness we carry around inside are pushed. If you press on the right bruise, anyone might push back defensively. In these situations, a calm head and some empathy can often return someone to their "right mind." All couples have experienced this: someone gets amped up and hurt, and the other one has the wherewithal to give some empathy and care and things get back to normal. *This is normal, common, and human.*

As Proverbs 15:1 says, "A gentle answer turns away wrath, but a harsh word stirs up anger" (NIV). Sometimes, when we respond to defensive anger that originates in hurt, softness really helps.

The "foolish" category we are discussing here is *not a momentary reactiveness. It is a stance whereby someone, in a significant area or the breakdown of trust, is unwilling to take responsibility for a problem and denies that there is a problem in an ongoing way.* When this happens, getting past it is difficult until something changes.

But I want to say that when you get a foolish, defensive, or denying reaction from someone, **it is not yet time to automatically give up hope.** Psychology and the Bible agree on this. I love the path described in Matthew 18:15-18. It is exactly the path that addiction specialists and others who deal with difficult behaviors have proven to be helpful. It begins with a one-on-one conversation and says that if someone owns what they have done, you have won them over and the problem is solved (v. 15). But if they do *not* own it, don't keep talking about it. They are not listening. At that point, bring in a couple of other people to help you with the conversation (v. 16). *Do not continue to talk to someone who is blaming you and being defensive by yourself.* The Bible and any good psychologist would advise to bring in a third party or a few people, and speak to the person together. It is much more difficult for someone to be defensive and continue to not take responsibility in the presence of a good marriage counselor, arbitrator, HR professional, or pastor or a few concerned friends in the room than with just you. Sometimes, several people speaking in one voice about an issue can break through denial.

Do not continue to talk to someone who is blaming you and being defensive by yourself.

If bringing a few people into the conversation doesn't work, a larger intervention is sometimes helpful, as the first part of Matthew 18:17 says and as addiction interventionists and others can attest.

The last step in this process is separation. As Matthew 18:17 or any good interventionist would tell you, if there is no ownership after one-on-one conversations, conversations with a small group, and then with a larger group, it's often time to separate from that person and hope that the consequences of losing connection will bring them to a remorseful place.

The bottom line for people who act foolishly and do not take responsibility for their behavior is to stop trying to get them to see it by yourself. Bring in help, maybe in increasing numbers. And, if all else fails, sometimes you might have to implement the consequence of no further contact until they are ready to listen. Sometimes when people experience a real "loss," it serves as a wake-up call because they do not want to lose everyone and everything that is important to them.

Evildoers

There is another category of people the Bible mentions and the legal system deals with in a totally different way than it deals with others, and that is "evil." While I won't go into the many perspectives on the origin or even the existence of evil, there is something worth mentioning here. No matter how you categorize certain behaviors and think about their possible healing, or change (and there are many different views), for our purposes in this book it's important to realize that there are some people who are not merely defensive or trying to avoid responsibility. *There are people who actually intend to hurt you.* Harm you. Destroy you. Or even kill you. This is reality, and dealing with this category of people, however you want to describe them, requires a different strategy, because you are actually in danger.

The Bible says that "evil" is categorized by the person's intent for destruction:

> *Don't envy evil people*
> *or desire their company.*
> *For their hearts plot violence,*
> *and their words always stir up trouble.*
> —Proverbs 24:1-2 NLT

There is a type of person who, when confronted, will "plot" violence and try to do something to hurt you. Whether it happens in the moment (think of a motorist who honks at another driver and then shoots at them or someone who physically attacks another person in a confrontation) or in a scenario where there is a longer plan or scheme (such as retaliatory lawsuits designed to bring down a company or an individual) or other hurtful revenge strategies, some **people are dangerous and really do want to harm the person with whom they have a conflict**. It happens every day.

You must go into protection mode with evil behavior.

The strategy for dealing with these individuals is **not** to engage and put yourself in danger and **not** to attempt to have a discussion or confrontation apart from whatever level of protection is needed. *You must go into protection mode with evil behavior.* Someone is trying to harm you, and that is not the moment to attempt reconciliation on your own. (This is why courtrooms have armed officers standing in the back of the room.)

This is where saying, "I'll only speak to you through my attorney. Call him at this number," and ending the conversation is needed. This is why people need to call 911 at times or why women sometimes need to seek a shelter and avoid a confrontation of any kind. Sometimes people just have to get to safety. As Proverbs 27:12 says, "A prudent person sees evil and hides himself; But the naive proceed, and pay the penalty" (NASB).

Be Wise

I can't overemphasize the importance of determining who you're dealing with as you figure out whether reconciliation is available in a broken trust situation. This will require conversations with the person who hurt you. As you attempt these conversations, regardless of what type of person the other one is, you be wise. Wisdom can make the difference between knowing whether to stop where you are, go forward just a little bit, move ahead in trust, or run for your life.

In Review

Before we move forward to the next chapter, let's review a few important points:

- Forgiveness is something you do inside your soul and does not require anything from the other person.
- Reconciliation can happen when someone says they are sorry, owns their behavior, and is genuinely repentant and remorseful. When it happens, you can move forward on good terms with each other. At this point, the other person has appropriated your forgiveness. You have reconciled after the conflict. Trust and having "more" in the relationship are not yet on the table at this point.
- *Reconciliation of a relationship does not mean you will trust the person moving forward.* That requires more than "I'm sorry." That trust will have to be earned.
- Reconciliation and/or repair of trust can only come from determining who the other person shows up to be. Are they now going to be trustworthy in the important ways that you have been learning throughout this book?

What About You?

We've been looking at determining who you're dealing with. The assumption has been that someone has actually done something wrong to you, misused trust in some way, and let you down. There truly is something to forgive, to try to reconcile, and to perhaps repair going forward.

But the fact that you or I was the one who was betrayed or let down does not automatically make us 100 percent innocent, mature,

208   T R U S T

or competent people. Sometimes we have some issues we need to look at too.

Before we go there, please hear what I am *not* saying. I am *not* saying that you caused the betrayal or the other person's failure. That is exactly what the defensive, blaming, gaslighting fool wants you to believe. Betrayal is a one-person act, as are the other personal issues the trust model addresses. If you have been hurt in those ways, it is not your fault or responsibility. Other people are responsible for their behavior. No victim blaming here.

What I'm talking about is basically your own health, strength, equipping, and maturity. While we will look at much of this in depth in a later chapter about reasons for misplaced trust, I do want to mention the issue of personal responsibility. We can learn all kinds of beneficial lessons from our broken trust experiences if we are willing to consider how we may have contributed to them. To trust well, we need to also look at ourselves and the abilities needed to trust well.

For example, we could learn a lot about our strengths and weaknesses and take steps to better utilize our strengths and bolster our weak areas. We could realize a tendency to micromanage others and begin to learn to delegate effectively. We may have to admit that we saw red flags in someone's behavior but ignored them because we don't like confrontation. We may need to work on our conflict resolution skills. Or, like Olivia, we may need to believe what we learn about someone in the reality of their untrustworthiness when it's been proven, and to take appropriate action promptly, even if we don't like it. Figuring out how we need to improve in broken trust situations will help us navigate our way through them and strengthen us as we go forward. It always behooves us to look at our side of every relationship in order to become the best we can be.

Becoming stronger, healthier, and wiser will help us hold people accountable to the process of repairing trust, as we shall see. All of us

need to be able to confront well, be wise in seeing and spotting deception, move beyond bitterness, and take other important growth steps.

**It's not your fault that someone else did what they did.
But it is always our responsibility to be our best, even in
dealing with difficult people.**

Remember, it's not your fault that someone else did what they
did. But it is always our responsibility to be our best, even in dealing with difficult people. I want you to be as strong and equipped as
you need to be.

Now That You Are Reconciled—or Not

At this point, you have taken care of yourself, have dealt with the past
injury, are healing your soul, have thought about what you want for
the future, and have addressed your relationship with the person who
let you down. You may be at the point where you have either parted
ways due to that person's ongoing denial or irreconcilable differences
based on their failure to take responsibility. Or, you may be at the
point where you want to look at moving forward. So, let's look at the
situation where you have determined that you do want to evaluate
repairing forward-moving in trust with the person, and let's look at
the next steps in that path forward.

SEVENTEEN

STEP 5: ASSESS TRUSTWORTHINESS TO DETERMINE IF TRUST IS AN OPTION, PART 1

After you've taken the first four steps in the process of repairing trust, it's time to take step 5 and determine whether the option of rebuilding trust with the person who betrayed you is viable. The way to do this is to use the five essentials of trust as a guide. These elements of trust are just as helpful in knowing if you can trust some- one *again* as they are in determining whether you can trust someone in the first place. They are the same. Trustworthiness elements are the same moving forward as they are in the beginning.

Before we take a fresh look at the five essentials of trust, this time in the context of repairing trust, let me tell you about a conversation I had with Drew. Remember him? He was Bella's husband, the attor- ney with the double life who betrayed his wife by having an ongo- ing affair with a work colleague, along with some other shenanigans.

Drew: The Model of the Model

As I reviewed the early chapters of this book and looked again at the five essentials of trust, I kept thinking of Bella and Drew. They have accomplished so much in repairing broken trust and rebuild- ing a marriage that is ten years past a major crisis and still thriving.

When I looked at the five essentials, I kept seeing a current picture of Drew in my mind's eye:

1. Understanding what the other person needs and how they feel
2. Having a motive and intent "for" the other person's welfare
3. Having the abilities and capacities to deliver what is promised
4. Having the character and personhood to meet the trust requirements
5. Building a track record that is a trustworthy pattern

I had to call him. He was the model of the model. I had worked with him and Bella from the beginning and gotten to follow them throughout the process of rebuilding their trust, their marriage and family, his career, and their life. The way they had engaged in the process was incredible, and I just wanted to tell Drew how inspired I was by what he had done over the years, as I had told Bella the last time I saw her.

When I explained this to Drew, he was surprised, and somewhat embarrassed, that I was extolling him as a hero. He began to protest, reminding me that the whole debacle had happened because he had screwed up—big time.

"True. You did screw up," I said. "But you've done everything it takes to put it back together. And I can honestly say that you are among the best models of it I have ever seen. I really mean that, and that's why I had to call you. You need to know that."

"Well, you are kind to call," he said. "I'll receive the encouragement."

"And, I'll say one more thing," I continued. "As I was writing about the trust model I've shared with you and Bella many times, what moved me most was remembering how well you performed in the first step—listening to her and understanding how everything affected her. You really listened and stuck in there while she shared some things that were hard for you to hear. You were never defensive. You just listened and cared, without saying anything to excuse, minimize, or blame. You just listened. It couldn't have been easy to take all of the hurt and anger pouring out at you. It was tough."

He was silent for a moment, and then he just said, "Wasn't easy."

We both laughed, realizing the profound truth and understatement of those two words. It was *not* easy, but he did it.

After that phone call with Drew, I thought it might be helpful to you to walk through the next part of their story so you can see how the model of repairing broken trust actually occurred.

As you read how Bella and Drew used the model to rebuild the trust between them, apply it to whatever context *you* are facing. For example, their story takes place in the context of a marriage relationship. But the same steps applied to Greg's business situation. He had to work with his partners *through these same steps*, as does anyone who is going to repair trust. The steps are what's important to see here, not just the specific ways that Bella and Drew applied them.

Starting Down the Path of Restored Trust

When Bella first found out about Drew's affair, you'll recall that she was devastated. She was broken, almost unable to get through each day for a while. She went from moments of numbness to crying spells to fits of rage in an unending cycle. Our first step was simply to try to help her get through the initial blows. We decided her best course of action was to take some time away from home and go to her sister's house in a nearby town. She was far enough to be able to get some needed space to fall apart, and close enough to do what she had to do with the kids.

Bella's sister was a great comfort to her, and the stability of having her sister and brother-in-law together provided some feeling

of security. With their support and the help of her individual therapist, she took one day at a time. I urged her not to think about making
any decisions, but just to get through each day. "The time to make
decisions will come," I assured her.

After that initial time, we met over multiple sessions to figure out
next steps. In short, it became clear that Drew was what, these days,
is called a sex addict. I felt he needed heavy limits, consequences,
confrontation, strict structure, and a therapeutic and spiritual approach
to help with the healing and rehabilitation he needed. A structured
team approach in a treatment center provided that, and he went.

A big reason our plan worked was that Bella held a hard line
regarding the consequence of the separation, and she refused to make
any commitments yet about the future. She had to heal first. Then
she needed to think about what she might want to do going forward,
instead of instantly accepting his apologies, as he begged her to put
their relationship and life back together.

As is the case with many people who are "caught," Drew really *was*
sorry, but his remorse seemed to be a mixture of "sorry" and "sorry he
got caught." He did not yet truly understand the pain he had caused,
nor was he fully broken by it. He simply wanted to *not* lose his entire
life as he knew it, though the threat of that was not an altogether bad
thing. It helped him hit bottom and realize he had some serious work
to do. He was scared. He should have been.

He was in the treatment center for a month, and he did a lot of
work. I was surprised at how powerfully he connected to the addict
model. It helped him admit he really was hopeless and powerless to
do better. Years of high-risk behavior had taught him this lesson, and
having others understand how powerless he really was really helped.
In the words of addiction circles, he was "working the program."

His treatment included marriage sessions and individual sessions,
along with group experiences and teaching. This gave Drew and Bella
a place to begin to process what had happened.

Without detailing everything that happened, suffice it to say that from there, Drew and Bella worked the first several steps of the model for repairing broken trust. We'll spend the remainder of the chapter looking at how this process unfolded for them.

Step 1: Heal from What Happened

Remember, healing from what happened to you includes getting to a place where you are emotionally and cognitively ready to move forward. Bella did this by going to her sister's and by staying connected to her small group from church, women she had met with for several years. That group included two women she was especially close to, and the three of them took walks together every morning. She also saw a therapist who helped her through a lot of the initial pain. She shared everything openly, which helped her immensely.

Drew pursued his own version of healing, even though he was the perpetrator of the offense. He was part of a group in rehab and then joined a sex addict group when he returned home. He also got an individual therapist and met with his pastor weekly. In addition, he built relationships with two new male friends who were in recovery themselves and provided help and support.

Step 2: Move Beyond Anger and Revenge and Turn Toward Forgiveness

Bella needed to work through her anger and turn toward forgiveness. This took a while, of course. She did it mainly through her individual therapy and her group. They gave her the space to process all that had happened to her. They didn't judge how she felt; they simply walked it through with her. While they all knew she had to get past the anger before anything good could happen, they did not "should" her about it. They helped her go at her own pace. Slowly, over time, she gained some acceptance of the situation, although it would be a while before it was neutralized. This is always a tough process.

Step 3: Ponder What You Really Want

Bella wanted both extremes from day one—to never have to trust Drew again, *and* to save her marriage and family. Processing those opposing wishes took time. She finally decided to face the possibility that her marriage could work again, and she began the process of moving in that direction. This was not easy, nor was it without a lot of staring reality in the face. She knew it would be work. She had to really own the fact that it would be difficult and also own the reality that she didn't want to lose everything she and Drew had together, if keeping it was possible. That desire kept her moving forward. Holding her family together was worth dealing with the pain and risk it required.

Step 4: Figure Out If Reconciliation Is Available

Remember, reconciliation does not automatically mean trust will be restored. It simply means getting to forgiveness and being okay with the person who hurt you. We discussed earlier that reconciliation requires figuring out where the other person is and determining whether they are remorseful, repentant, and apologetic. For Bella, figuring out that Drew was indeed truly sorry and repentant was not difficult. It was clear that he had hit bottom. Bella also saw how he listened and participated in the sex addict recovery program. He complied with everything asked of him and was openly remorseful and confessional with Bella. He was not defensive, nor did he blame her.

While this step was relatively easy for Bella, in some situations it is difficult and confusing. Excusing, blaming, and lack of true repentance are big barriers to reconciliation, and they must be addressed until everyone close to the situation feels that the person is truly sorry and owns what they have done. As long as they are blaming and excusing, they are not fully ready, and reconciliation is difficult. Repentance happens without blaming the other party in any way. There will be ample time later to work on mutual issues in the relationship and to work toward improving it.

Step 5: Determine If Trust Is an Option

Remember, determining if trust is an option after reconciliation requires working through the five essentials of trust anew. If you are going to trust someone again, then it must work like all trust works: the essentials must be there. I want you to see how Bella and Drew did this:

Understanding

Drew began to listen to Bella's pain and hurt, and he only listened, at least in the beginning. He did everything he could to understand not only what she had gone through with his betrayal, but also to begin making a concerted effort to understand her real needs in the total relationship. She needed to feel confident about the answers to these questions:

- Does he understand what is important to me?
- Does he understand what I need from him?
- Does he really get what makes me feel open and careless with him, and what will make me move toward him in trust? Can he show the ability to really hear me in my feelings?
- Does he understand me, my reality, and my desires in our relationship?

In the beginning of their process, Bella mostly needed Drew to hear what he had done to her and how it affected her, to be aware of the pain he had caused. Doing this is *so* difficult. No one naturally wants to listen to all the ways that they have hurt or disappointed someone. It is hard to listen to our failures and hear the pain we have caused someone, and take in their anger and hurt. It's difficult for a person to just sit and listen to those things without excusing himself or herself, or without saying, "Well, I did that because you weren't meeting my needs," or making some other excuse. But it is always necessary to sit and listen.

The one who has done the offending must begin the process with really listening to the myriad ways they have hurt the other person and let them down without defending or minimizing.

This first step to healing is so hard for many people. There is so much shame and guilt that they want to defend themselves, but they do better to simply listen and empathize. I wish I had a dollar for every time I have said to the offender, in situations like Drew and Bella's, "Just be quiet and listen."

Beyond listening to Bella, Drew had to begin to understand that, for a long time, *she had needed to be able to tell him when she was hurt or where her needs were not addressed, and have him hear it instead of taking it as criticism.* He had to understand that her talking to him about issues did not mean she was "against" him but that she needed him. She needed him to understand that she wanted to be able to share things with him without his getting defensive.

Bella also needed Drew to understand that being provided for was not the only way she felt loved. He saw himself as taking good care of the family and their needs because he worked hard, but Bella needed some emotionally focused attention, just being together. He had to learn to really hear that for the first time and show that he understood.

As an ongoing practice for quite a while, Drew had to listen when Bella got triggered about his betrayal. When feelings of how it still affected her surfaced, he had to listen again to things he thought he had listened to many times (and he had) and understand that *expressing the pain once didn't heal it for her.* Pain often has to be "sponged out" through multiple expressions over time. But, the more Drew listened and understood, the more Bella's pain got expressed—and diminished. He had to understand this paradox: expression brings about less expression. Listen, and expressed pain will decrease over time, as understanding heals it.

Overall, Drew demonstrated to Bella that his stance was to always truly understand what she needed from him and to listen more deeply in general.

Motive

Drew had to prove to Bella that his motive and intent were for her good and for the good of their relationship. Bella had always wrestled with the feeling that her good and the good of their marriage were not Drew's most important motives. While she knew he was invested in the relationship in some ways, she felt she came in second or third to his real motives, *which were about himself.* When she thought about it, she realized that they used most of their time and resources to please him. He did some things that were important to her, *but when they conflicted with his desires, she didn't seem to be his first priority.* That had to change for trust to be repaired.

But Drew learned, and he did a great job of showing Bella that he would be motivated first for her good and the good of their relationship—before his own interests. She needed to feel their marriage took priority over his career or anything else.

Drew learned to ask himself before doing anything, "How would this feel to Bella? How would this affect her?" This was huge in the trust repair process. He began, for instance, to include her in decisions about whether to make certain business trips or take on a case that would require more time away from the family. He stopped simply informing her when he planned to play golf or pursue other personal interests and began including her in decisions about how to spend his time. If his job called for meetings, events, or business relationships that made her uncomfortable, he either did not engage in them or they found a way to make them feel better to her. For example, he started including other people in meetings or gatherings so he would not be in compromising situations. The biggest behavior of this point was this: **He learned to question himself before doing anything, by saying, "How would this feel to her? How would this affect her?"**

One very big aspect of showing "intent" was before doing anything that would make her feel uncomfortable in terms of his travels or other times away from her. He also took additional steps to show that his intent was not only to remain faithful, but to help Bella know how he was doing it. He planned his trips with her and gave her full access to his communications, with tracking software to check his texts, calls, and locations if she wanted. His intent was to fully live his life in the open, being fully transparent with her. He showed her that intent completely.

Drew also demonstrated that, where his sex addiction was concerned, *his motive was to get well*. He pursued his recovery, his therapy, and their couples therapy wholeheartedly. He read books, listened to audio material, went to his meetings, talked with his sponsor, and did everything he needed to do to show that his intent was to get well and stay well. *Bella did not have to guess whether or not he was serious*. When there was a conflict between his sobriety work and his work, if possible, he moved the professional obligation, revealing that his growth and commitment to the marriage and faithfulness was first priority. All of this contributed to Bella's confidence that Drew was thinking about her and their marriage. She came to believe he was "for" her, not just for himself.

Ability

Bella needed to see Drew developing some new abilities that were crucial for her to trust him again. These abilities fell into two categories: relational abilities and personal ability for sexual self-control. These were the two areas in which trust had been broken.

Relationally, Drew worked in their marriage counseling to learn communication and conflict resolution skills that were key to Bella's feeling close to him. During conflict, he had always communicated in a defensive and domineering way, trying to convince her that he was right, instead of listening to where she was coming from. He had to learn some new skills in that regard to make her feel connected. He also had to learn to validate what she was feeling before trying to talk her out of it, essentially to stop gaslighting her. And, he had to learn to not disconnect from her when he felt hurt or upset with her. Instead of disconnecting from her in a conflict by rolling his eyes and walking out, then medicating himself with some sexual liaison, he had to learn to turn *into* the relationship instead of away from it when things did not feel good. He learned to move *toward* Bella in conflict instead of *away from* or *against* her.

In terms of staying faithful, Drew had to learn the skills of recovery, sexual sobriety, and faithfulness. Watching him do this diligently through calling his sponsor, meeting consistently with his group, and pursuing his spiritual growth helped Bella immensely. She saw him become an "expert" in how his addiction and problems worked and an expert in managing his life. These were new abilities for him, and he worked at them diligently. His efforts reminded Bella of his approach to his professional life: "In it to win it." But this time it was for life and for them.

Drew knew the skill of staying connected to his recovery group was vital, and every Monday morning, in addition to everything else he was doing, he had a ninety-minute weekly conference phone call with them. He demonstrated that he was developing *sobriety ability*, and that was huge for Bella to see. No matter what he or they were doing, he would not miss that call for any reasonably avoidable reason, nor would he miss any of his other growth activities.

Character

There were a few areas where Drew really had to show Bella that he was growing in character. One was *honesty and transparency*. He had always been disconnected in some ways. He maintained a certain privacy, call it "secrecy," about his finances, his schedule, his whereabouts, and his activities. Answers such as, "Oh, I was just in a meeting," were no longer okay. Not sharing complete financial information with Bella was no longer okay. *He had to develop more openness and full-blown honesty and transparency that gave no opportunity for duplicity.* He gave Bella full access to his calendar, phone, and computer, along with all of their finances. When she began to feel that what she saw was all there was, trust became more and more possible, and eventually, even easy.

Another area in which Drew grew was his ability to be emotionally present with Bella. Previously, his lack of patience and seeming inability to live in the moment were big barriers to her feeling truly connected to him. As he increased in his ability to be present and connected to her, she was able to rest more and more in feeling safe and cared for by him. She no longer felt she was always chasing him, never quite able to catch up with him, and they could simply sit and "be." Safety needs connection, and connection is built through presence. He put down his device during dinners, for example.

Lastly, Bella saw Drew develop humility as it related to accountability. He had always basically kept his own counsel, not really answering to anyone else. That had made her nervous, and she later discovered she'd been right to worry about it. But now, with new accountability to sponsors, a group, therapists, and even his law partners, that was changing. He was submitting to others and receiving their input in healthy accountable relationships.

Track Record

Drew was impressive in creating a new track record. He attended everything he committed to—all his recovery meetings and all marriage and personal counseling sessions. He didn't miss sessions "here and there," which almost invariably turns into a pattern. Track records are building blocks of all trust.

Drew established track records in relating to Bella as well, as they had more and more conversations in which he *proved* to be non-defensive and open, connecting, and present. She could feel his changing over time. The track record was working, slowly convincing her over time that the good things that were happening were real.

Certainly, Drew had some "misses" along the way as he undertook the process of changing so trust could be restored. That happens in life. But what's important is that the patterns were all strong and trending in the right direction: he was changing and committed. You could see it in a graph if you made one: up and to the right.

EIGHTEEN

STEP 6: ASSESS TRUSTWORTHINESS TO DETERMINE IF TRUST IS AN OPTION, PART 2

Remember the Foreigner song "Feels Like the First Time"? Mentioning a 1970s love song here may seem cheesy, but in a sense, the words of the song title are exactly what we are discussing. When you attempt to repair trust, obviously you aren't trusting the person for the first time, because you have already trusted him or her before. But actually, you are trusting them for the first time in a different way, because this time it will be based on the five essentials of trust. And it can feel very different, like it's *real* for the first time.

When there is a breakdown in trust, a review of the relationship usually shows that the elements never were truly present in full. One or more of them failed, or were too weak. And because of that, your repaired trust will often be *the "first time" the essentials of trust have fully been at work in the relationship.*

Often, when people look back on a broken trust situation, as Bella did, *they see huge gaps in the relationship over time in one or more of the five essentials*: **understanding, motive, ability, character, and track record**. But the gaps went unnoticed, or someone didn't pay attention to them, or they were overlooked or not given the weight they should have had. Many times it had been too fearful to address them.

But when those elements are finally present in the repair season, you feel you've opened up a door (as the Foreigner song says) to real trust. It really is often the first time. The key to this is making sure that this time, all five essentials are present and that you feel confident about each one. This is why we often hear, in a repaired relationship, "we have something now we never had before."

In the previous chapter, we looked at some specific ways Bella and Drew began to repair their marriage after a trust crisis, based on the five essentials. In other contexts, such as business, the repair path is the same. You'll still rely on the five essentials you've come to know over the course of this book. You'll look for them and be able to see them every step of the way.

If we think about Greg's story, when Rob ended up with the company he started and loved because one of Greg's partners sold out to Rob, in many ways his business partnership was missing the same five elements that Bella and Drew had to work through. The partner who betrayed him never understood how much more important the mission of the company was to Greg than profits. To be fair, Greg may have downplayed the necessity of profits more than he realized. He was all about the mission, while the others wanted him to worry more, as they did, about the finances. He didn't understand their need very well either.

But Greg and the people around him entered "trust repair" mode after they realized that they wanted to try to keep the business together. And they had to walk through the same process that Bella and Drew did in the marriage arena. *They had to listen to each other to really **understand** what was important to each side—mission, relationships, culture, and finances, to name a few.* They had to align their **motives** with a transparent goal and vision that lifted both sides to something higher than themselves and their own interests, and they had to be "for" what other people needed, not just what they needed themselves. In terms of **abilities,** each side had to develop new skills and capacities to fulfill the new roles they were entrusted with. They also had to surrender some areas in which they did not have the abilities the other side needed. In other words, they had to realize that they could not ask for trust in ways they were not equipped to deliver. For example, Greg did not have some of the operational capacities the new partners had, and he had to relinquish some of those responsibilities so they could trust him in his areas of strength and not be disappointed when he didn't perform well at things he simply wasn't good at performing.

In the **character** and personal makeup arenas, everyone involved had to work on being fully forthcoming and totally transparent with each other. This meant no more shielding each other from what one department or partner did because of their own interests or passions without the knowledge of the other side. It also meant complete transparency in all financial dealings. When questioned, all defensiveness and blaming and suspiciousness had to be left behind. Everyone's financials had to be transparent. Total access, all the time.

As time went on, and they continued to work in our process with my structuring their work around these issues, they were establishing a **track record.** In each conversation, they were able to build on the previous one, and it went well. Then they could trust that the next conversation would go well too.

During many of my sessions with them, there were times I thought everything might fall apart. There was so much water under the bridge and mistrust was in the air. But the more they focused and really worked on the five essentials, the more the trust was repaired. Ultimately, they continued to work together for a long time, and very successfully. But this would have never happened had they not addressed these specific elements as they repaired trust. Those five essentials of the model were key to their long-term success in working together.

Remember, when *doing the actual repair work*, the first task is to bring the five essentials of trust into full view in the relationship as the people involved look forward. To begin, *review the relationship and see where any of the five elements of trust may have been missing, so both parties will know where the trust broke down*:

- Where was there the lack of "understanding"? Where did the one who betrayed trust not understand what their partner in the trust relationship needed? What was not being understood, validated, and attended to?
- Where were they acting with "motives" and "intent" that other people felt were self-focused? How did they fail to take the other party into consideration? Remember, the basic definition of a betrayal is when one party acts in their own interests without thinking of what the other party needs. Where was that happening?
- What abilities may have been assumed but were actually lacking in the person who betrayed the other one? How did this lead to disappointment, injury, or hurt? Can those abilities be built or is there a need to reassign some roles or areas of trust?
- What personal character issues hurt the relationship and should be addressed? How did those issues hurt the other person or the other side? Are those issues now understood? Is the person owning them and focusing on them as the two sides discuss what went wrong?
- What was the real track record in the areas of broken trust, disappointment, or failure?

When the parties have explored and understood all of the above, they must ask this question:

Is trust an option going forward? Is everyone willing to behave in specific ways in these five essential areas?

- Understanding
- Motive
- Ability
- Character
- Track Record

The parties must be specific as to how each of these elements will be lived out in the relationship going forward. What does each of these require and what are the expectations?

Get Help

As you do the work of repairing trust, my strong suggestion is to figure out in the very beginning *who will help you in this process?* In order to work on the five elements, most repair journeys that are successful enlist the right help from outside, meaning outside of the relationship. In fact, having some people to help you walk the path is required.

There are a million possibilities for help, and all are valid: counselors, mentors, coaches, therapists, consultants, trainings, developmental performance paths, board interventions, wise people in your church or community, and others.

When you think about it, even good parents do all five of our trust essentials on an ongoing basis as they raise their children, so there is no one way to develop into being a trustworthy person. The elements are always the same, but whatever path you take to address them, you must make sure there is sufficient structure to the process and that you have outside help to make sure it gets done. What I'm saying is: *The two parties directly involved in the breakdown of trust usually cannot restore it by themselves.* They need outside parties who show up and bring three ingredients to the repair process:

1. *Outside support*

The path of repairing trust will be rocky. There will be hurt
feelings, conflict, and discouragement. There must be people
on the outside who can support both parties when they feel
the work is "just too hard." Drew needed his sponsor, therapist, group, and me to help him overcome the feelings that he
had failed too miserably and would never be able to do enough.
Bella needed to be encouraged at times that it truly was possible for him to get better, and that minor setbacks were not the
end of their journey. Greg needed his board and me, another
consultant, and his partners to move past his hurt and see the
bigger picture to continue moving forward.

Again, repairing trust is very difficult at times. Just as
members of a Navy SEAL team have to pick each other up
along the way, or a physical therapist has to push someone
through the pain to get strong again, people need multiple
forces of support for a broken relationship to get over the painful, fearful, and energy-draining bumps in the road toward
restored trust.

2. *Outside intelligence*

There will be many unknowns on the path toward restored
trust. Drew had no clue how to rebuild trust, and Bella didn't
know how to explain it and get him to engage. It took the
wisdom, knowledge, and experience of addiction counselors,
the marriage therapist, others, and me to help them know what
to do and to learn new skills. They needed to find out what
was normal in the process, and what was an expected difficulty
versus what was a horrible violation everyone should scream
about. Both of them needed to be coached and corrected along
the path to know what was okay and what wasn't.

New skills and ways of being together are necessary to make any relationship better. While the betrayal of trust is always the responsibility of the one who betrays, both parties usually need to grow in certain ways of being in the relationship. Again, this is not in any way to blame the victim or say their behavior "causes" the bad behavior of another. *But the overall goal is for both parties to have a different and better relationship than they had before. Certainly, neither is perfect and both can learn to help each other as they work together.* This requires some learning, and outside intelligence is needed. Even the victim must learn new ways to be empowered to intervene or get help if something does not look good so that she or he will not be wounded again.

Whatever your context—marriage and family, business, or some other area of life—bring into the mix people who can help you, whether they are in professional roles, such as counselors, coaches, or consultants, or in personal roles, such as mentors or wise friends. Usually, both are needed, but the bottom line is that new ways, new wisdom, and intelligence must be brought into the situation. As Albert Einstein said, "The thinking that got us to where we are is not the thinking that will get us to where we want to be."* Get around some people who have some "new thinking."

3. *A structured path*

Trust repair does not happen on the fly, when it's convenient, or when people have extra time on their hands. There must be a structure to the process. Basically, to provide *structure* means to add a frame of how something is going to happen, who

---

* Albert Einstein, AZQuotes.com, Wind and Fly LTD, n.d., https://www.azquotes.com /quote/823642.

plays what role in the process, when and where things will take place, and what the activities will be. The word *structure* means "the action of building"[*] (think of a building as a "structure"), and the process we are discussing is one of rebuilding trust. It won't happen without the proper scaffolding, so to speak, in place while trust is reconstructed. You need a lattice to grow a beautiful vine.

In my consulting work, for example, one of the first items I discuss with a client is what the structure will be. How often will we meet? Who will be involved? Will it be just the CEO (or whichever leader is the focus), or will the meetings include her team or bigger parts of the company, or possibly the entire entity? Will the board participate? What part will each person play? What will we need each one to do to make this work? How will we evaluate how we are doing? As we answer these questions, we erect the structure necessary for rebuilding trust. All of that provides the rails to keep the train moving.

Think about this: had Drew and Bella or Greg not had a structured process, they all would have failed. Had there not been a meeting in place, at a specific time, that Drew was required to attend, discouragement or lack of courage would have kept him from getting in the right mood to go talk to someone who would help him on a particular day. What if he and Bella hadn't had a marriage counseling appointment that he would have to go to, knowing that being with her would involve hearing a lot of hurt and anger directed at him? Canceling that conversation might have been easy, had it not been a real appointment that was already scheduled and required. What if others had not been observing his track record and

---

[*] "Structure," Merriam-Webster, updated November 5, 2022, https://www.merriam-webster.com/dictionary/structure.

holding him accountable to participate in the process of repairing trust? Discouragement might have overtaken him—and/or Bella—along the way.

Structure matters. Don't leave it up to a kid to decide when bedtime is or where to sleep. You have to have a time and a place where bedtime happens or you will never see maturity and change occur. From NFL athletes to surgeons-in-training to addicts in recovery, everyone has to show up to the scheduled practice sessions. We all need structure in our lives to get to the next place.

As you try to repair trust personally or professionally, not only must the five essentials of trust gain focus, they must gain focus in a structured way and in many little ways. For example, when working with executive teams, at the end of every meeting, I have them work through a structure to ask themselves how well they lived up to the behavioral values they promised to abide by. I have them build in the structure of reviewing at the end of every meeting and grade themselves, even for a few minutes. Little structures build new ways of being, and big structures provide a path that takes people where they need to go.

The Five Essentials Road Map for Your Situation

I mentioned earlier that people trying to repair trust need to look at the five essentials through the rearview mirror, meaning in hindsight, to better understand how those elements of trust were violated. Both parties need to see where understanding, motive, ability, character, and track record broke down. After that happens, *the real work begins, the work of doing things differently going forward. The rearview mirror shows us where we went wrong, but a map forward shows us how to get where we need to go.*

It's time for you to draw your own road map to the future of your marriage, family relationship, business, or other area of life that has suffered because of broken trust. In collaboration with your outside help, begin to define each area in your relationship or partnership, using the five essentials of trust. As you answer the questions in each category, you'll define what is needed to build and sustain trust:

Understanding

- What is essential to you for the other party to really hear and understand for you to feel you can put your heart, or wallet, into their hands again? What essential needs of yours must be understood and met for you to trust again? Where do you really need the other person or party to listen, and what do you need them to get?
- What specific behaviors will you need to see to begin to feel secure that they are listening and understanding?
- What specific behaviors that would destroy your feeling that the other person is listening and understanding will you need to *not* see? For example, ignoring checking in? Invalidation? Trying to talk you out of how you feel instead of understanding it? Minimizing? Unplugging from conversations? Judging or criticizing your needs?

Motive

- What do you need to see from the other person to prove that their intention takes your welfare into consideration? What shows you they are looking out for your interests as well as their own? Which of those interests matter most to you? What makes you feel like they are "for" you and want the best for you?
- What specific behaviors will you need to see to demonstrate the other person's motives?
- What specific behaviors will you need to *not* see?

Ability

- What competencies do you need to depend on in this relationship? Are they actually present or can they be built? Have you considered the personal and professional abilities that are necessary to make it work (such as communication skills, for example)?

- Do you need to reassign some roles in order to avoid a breakdown in trust? For example, maybe one person is terrible at managing money, but the other one is good at it, so that one should handle the finances. Or in a business relationship, the partnership or team may not need to rely on a certain person to fulfill a particular responsibility because that person doesn't excel in that area, but could be depended on to do something else because they are great at it.

- What relationship skills and abilities or emotional intelligence are absolutely necessary to make the relationship work well? How will those be addressed?

- How will you define success in those areas? What results or behaviors will you look for?

Character

- What aspects of personhood will you need to experience in order to trust the other person? Impulse control? Patience? Perseverance? Kindness? Lack of defensiveness? Compassion?

- Does the person possess those traits? If not enough, how will you address the growth process as they develop those qualities?

- How will you address failures along the way? For example, if you are rebuilding financial trust and someone overspends one month, what will happen? What if an impulsive partner or executive falls in love with a new business deal that derails the plan everyone on the team had agreed to?

- What behaviors do you want to see in the area of character and personal makeup?
- What behaviors do you *not* want to see?

Track Record

- How will the process of repairing trust be monitored? What cadence or timing will be expected as you move forward?
- Who will determine the pace at which you move forward? The two of you? The outside help? The team?

As you follow your road map to a better future, it's important to monitor and *celebrate progress*! For sure, lack of a good track record is significant, as it indicates a problem. But establishing a good track record is what building trust is all about, and the one who has to trust must acknowledge at some point that the other person or party has changed in order to keep things moving in a positive direction. At times, it is difficult for the betrayed person to admit the reality of change, but essential. If they don't, it can make the one who is changing very discouraged.

Over the past several chapters, we've looked extensively at how trust is rebuilt. You prepared to rebuild it by healing from what happened to you, working through anger, turning toward forgiveness, and pondering what you really want. You determined where the other person was and figured out that reconciliation was possible. You also reviewed how the five essentials of trust broke down in the past and defined how they will be lived out moving forward. *Then you begin to watch for those elements being displayed anew.*

At this point, both parties have seen how trust was broken and specifically defined what it will take to fix it. Now, it is about doing the work and putting the final key in place to help with the scariness of uncertainty:

How do you know if you can trust the process of change to be real and dependable?

That's what we'll focus on in the next chapter.

NINETEEN

STEP 7: LOOK FOR EVIDENCE OF REAL CHANGE

The big question, and the one that most troubles people in the process of repairing trust is this: "Should I keep going?" They simply want to know if they truly can trust the change process the other person has engaged in, and whether it will be fruitful. They don't want to be hurt or betrayed again.

Know this: no one can predict the future. There are no guarantees that the other person will always be trustworthy. The only one who can assure trustworthiness in the future is the one who broke the trust in the past. That's right, the person who broke your trust decides whether or not to earn your trust going forward. Their behavior will make the determination. All you need to do is to observe it, to watch it from the bleachers, so to speak. You do not have to be a fortune teller. You have to be an observer of their behavior.

Eleven Indicators of True Change

There are many ways to look for genuine change in a person. In this chapter, let's focus on eleven identifiable, objective criteria to watch for as you determine whether someone really meant it when they promised to change. If the person is sincere, you will see evidence of that sincerity in working their path of change, as seen in these indicators. Of course, the five essentials of trust are the *behavioral changes you are looking for in order to trust again*. But these eleven indicators of engagement in the true change process you'll read about in this chapter will help you watch how sincerely they are pursuing getting better in the five essentials. They will show you how to monitor a person's attempts to change and see if they are serious about changing or not.

So, to be clear: trust depends on the five essentials. How hard they are trying to get better can be seen by observing these eleven indicators of true engagement.

1. *Admission of Need*

When someone truly realizes they have some issues they need to change, they admit it and are open to receiving help. They say, "I need to get better at _____, and I need help to do it." Certainly they do need help, or you wouldn't have had a trust issue with them to begin with, right? But *your* being aware of this and *their* being aware of it are two different things. When they voice it, it indicates a teachable, hungry-to-change, listening and learning posture.

It is always encouraging to hear someone say, "I need some help because I'm just not good at that," or "I have trouble telling the truth sometimes. I don't know why, but I need someone to help me figure it out," or "I need some help with my drinking. I can't control it. I see that now." Or even in the skills department, "I need some coaching or training to get better at that. I can see how I fail people and I understand why they are upset with me."

In this first indicator of true change, you are primarily looking for someone to admit, "I have a problem and I need help." Expecting someone to change on their own isn't reasonable. If an issue is big enough to have broken your trust, they most often need help to change it. When you hear them owning the issue and owning their need for some kind of help, that is humility. And humility is the bedrock of change. Without it, growth can't happen because arrogance and a lack of need prevents any change from happening. If I do not need it, then obviously, it won't happen. This is why Jesus said, "Blessed are the poor in spirit, for theirs is the kingdom of heaven" (Matt. 5:3 NIV). When we realize we are poor and in need, then good things can be given to us. If we have no need, we, de facto, don't change.

If someone is open to getting help, that is a good sign. Sometimes they might not even know that help is available, and it has to be pointed out to them. But, when it is, they will be open to receiving it, knowing that they have the need to get better and desire to get there. "Blessed are those who hunger and thirst for righteousness, for they will be filled" (Matt. 5:6 NIV).

When people are changing, there is some process that is bringing that about, other than their own willpower.

---

2. Verifiable Involvement in a Proven Change Process

When people are changing, there is some process that is bringing that about, other than their own willpower. They are involved in some change path that chances are, they did not invent, and that has been proven over and over. If an alcoholic says, "Oh, yeah. Bob down at the church said he will meet with me and be my accountability partner to stop drinking too much," then hit STOP. "Bob's Treatment Program" has no track record or proven experience in helping people get sober. If someone is financially irresponsible, to have them buy a workbook on making a budget is not going to work. If a person has a history of being a difficult team member on a work team and just says he is going to "do better," then I would not have a lot of hope.

But, if instead of "Bob's Treatment," the alcoholic says they have a sponsor and are going to work the program with AA, or check in to a reputable treatment center, those are proven change processes. If a person says that they are going to get an experienced financial counselor, or join a Dave Ramsey group program, then that is something we will get excited about in having hope for their finances. If the difficult team member hires a reputable executive coach with a proven track record, then we might think some change is possible.

What you want to know when someone takes steps toward change is: Is this process known? Has it built a track record of helping people in the ways this person needs to change? If the person is working with an individual, such as a counselor or a mentor, find out about their credentials. Ask whether they are working with a proven, evidence-based methodology and not something they personally came up with. Ask about the counselor's or mentor's track record.

It is amazing how much well-intentioned "help" people sign up for when they might as well be using a divining rod. And since we are talking about trust, ask yourself, "Do I trust the process this person is using to become trustworthy?'"

Often, people want to design their own path for getting better. Many times, they want to be in charge of the process themselves, without submitting to the requirements of a professional path toward change. People with narcissistic or entitled personalities frequently think they know better than the professionals. But the willingness to submit to the demands of a proven program often signals whether it's reasonable to hope for a good outcome. This does not mean that you can't be flexible. Sometimes the one chosen that is proven is not right for that person, and a change to another counselor or program is needed. But, it should be a change that is credible.

3. *A Structured Approach*

Actually making significant changes in behavior or in one's approach to a relationship or business usually requires a *structured* approach. A structure may include showing up for appointments, attending groups, receiving coaching, completing assignments, or other activities that aid the process of change. And it is a great indicator of how serious the person is. *As I referred to earlier, the structure guides the acquisition and development of new skills that are not yet self-sustaining.* Think of it as a lattice for a bush, or scaffolding for a building being built. Or training wheels for someone riding a bicycle. Or boot camp for building the skills and disciple of a new soldier, or "two a day" practices for a football team over the summer. It is also a great indicator of how serious the person is, whether or not they will submit to the structure that a process requires in showing up for appointments, groups, coaching, etc.

When I worked in treatment centers, we required addicts to attend "90 meetings in 90 days," or some other similar structure. Structure is so important in making sure the right patterns are established and the right protections from slips and backsliding are in place. Just as a brace keeps a broken leg in place while it gets strong and gains the ability to stand on its own again, structure enables people to build new skills, patterns, and capacities. Even in the business world, someone receiving coaching should have a structure with time and place and specific activities to submit to.

Remember, structure involves time, place, persons, roles, activities, monitoring, discipline, consequences, and the like—*external* requirements guide the process of change. If a person won't agree to doing what they are supposed to do, you likely have a problem.

The structure doesn't have to be inflexible or unchangeable. Things happen. But the principle here is what Jesus taught when he healed someone on the Sabbath. The Sabbath was a day, a structure, when no work was to be done to build a good life. It was to be adhered to regularly. Yet, someone needed healing and Jesus healed them on the Sabbath, breaking the structure. When He was criticized for it, His response was so profound: "The Sabbath was made for man, not man for the Sabbath" (Mark 2:27 NIV). This teaches us so much about structure. It exists for us. We need it *to become what we are intended to be*. It is there to serve us. If it isn't working or should be altered for some reason, it's okay to change it for a good reason. But remember, it is very important and it's there for the benefit of the person who needs it.

Do not assume someone will change without some structure to help them do it. When someone needs to build new behaviors and capacities, it will take a structure to help them, and you will do well to look for it being present, and adherence to it from the bleachers.

4. *Skilled Help*

While "skilled help" may seem a bit like the "proven change" process, it digs a little deeper. Sometimes in a proven process, such as a treatment center or a leadership development program, the particular skills the person needs are present, but you can't assume they are all that this person needs or right for them. A program may be proven, but still lacking something important for *this* person.

Some structured programs may use a cookie-cutter approach that does not provide the particular expertise needed in a particular situation. It's good to know if the program and the personnel will provide the specific expertise and focus the person needs.

I am often asked by a CEO client, a company, or a family to interview an agency and find out if the skills are present, to evaluate the treatment before they sign on. Among other things, I look for areas of expertise, the personality of the counselors, areas in which the counselors have worked and been successful, and whether the center is better at some types of help than others. Sometimes you have to drill down to the specifics of an expert's particular orientation. All surgeons might do knee surgery, but what if this person needs robotic or minimally invasive, or vice versa? Both are proven, but not right for this particular case. The counselor or executive coach may provide couples counseling or CEO coaching, but are they strong enough to handle a particularly aggressive narcissist? The client or family and I just want to know that the skills needed for a certain problem are present, that *the help we need is going to be there.*

This doesn't apply only to mental health professionals. In most turnaround situations, other people are part of the picture too—bosses, HR professionals, pastors, mentors, friends, and more. But when someone is in a specific crisis, such as a trust betrayal, make sure each person involved brings real skills to the party. Warm bodies are not enough. In these journeys, it is good to have people with some kind of experience, talent, wisdom, or expertise alongside the professionals to provide other types of input and help. Who is invited to help and what are they bringing to the game?

5. *New Experience and Skills*

In a change process, obviously, new skills are needed. The person's previous personal and interpersonal skills are not working, and part of the change process is the development of new skills and competencies. The person should be able to say they are learning some new skills in various areas needed for them. Some examples might be: listening, communication, conflict resolution, time management, sobriety, community building, team building, delegation, submission to authority, anxiety and stress management, life management, emotional regulation, mindfulness, assertiveness, empathy training, or others that apply. These or other competencies might be required for the person to function in new ways.

Obviously, we all need improvement in many of these categories, so we're not looking for someone to be proficient in every possible life skill or work skill. *What we are looking for is an emphasis on specific skills the person is developing that are directly connected to the trust failure they were involved in.* We want some sort of personal and interpersonal growth to point to to say, "Wow! This is good for him or her to learn. I'm glad they are focusing on that. That will help."

6. *Self-Sustaining Motivation*

I cannot say enough about this indicator of true change. If someone (including you) has to prod the person to go to their counselor or coach or sessions or whatever, and they might not do it without your pushing them, it's often a bad sign. As Jesus said, "Blessed are those who hunger and thirst for righteousness, for they shall be filled" (Matt. 5:6 NIV). If the person is going to change, at some point, it will probably be because *they* want to change and vigorously pursue change with their own effort. Circumstances do push many people to change. And often we really do have to push push push to get it going. But for the change process to be sustained, it needs the push to shift from others to the person needing the change. It has to become self-motivated.

If someone really wants to change, they go after it. No one has to continually talk them into it. This doesn't mean someone may not need a lot of encouragement in the beginning or some support to stay involved when they hit rough spots along the way. People often need help starting and support to continue and to get grounded. Many want to quit. Some even drop out and need to be rescued and pushed back in. But a steady pattern of having to drive the change process for someone else that continues for a long time is a bad sign. You can lead a horse to water . . .

I've learned a surprising lesson over the years as a CEO and performance coach. When I first started this kind of work, I thought the lesser performers and the people struggling would most utilize my help. I expected the majority of the calls in between sessions to come from them, not the highest performers. *But the opposite has been true over the decades.* The stellar, world-class performers are the ones who tend to call me the most. They *want* input. They *want* feedback on how they are doing. They *want* opinions on people and situations before acting. They *crave* and seek help on their own. They are examples of the wise person we discussed earlier. They are humble and hungry, and as a result, they get better and better. But no one has to push them to call. They do it on their own.

7. *The Presence of Support*

I have mentioned the need for specific kinds of help in coaching, counseling, mentoring, and other settings that help people change. Certainly, they provide a lot of support. But people trying to make significant changes also need just good old-fashioned support from people who are just there for them as friends and cheerleaders. People need encouragement and to feel that someone is in their corner.

Make sure that whoever you are watching in process of change has a few close confidants who are aware of what is going on and can just be there as a good support person, listener, encourager, and safety net. Change does not happen in isolation. The people who do best in the change process have a "tribe" or a "village" to support them along the way. Trying to do it alone gets tough.

I love to see my clients have a strong support system because I know support systems keep people on track and even accelerate the process. Usually, all the needed support won't come from the "betrayed party," as they are dealing with their own pain. It's needed from outside circles.

Change is a process, and it is going to take time.

---

8. *Some Evidence of Change*

Nothing gets better in a day. Change is a process, and it is going to take time. But you do want to see some movement, even if perfection is still a long way away. This doesn't even have to mean that someone is "better" soon. It may mean they seem worse, in the sense that they may be in more pain or hit bottom, for example. What's important is that *something is happening over time.* We want to see change in some direction, shifts taking place, new patterns forming, and other developments. We want to hear the person talking about learning or experiencing something *new.* If more of the same is all we see, over a significant period of time, we should question whether anything is happening or not.

9. *Monitoring Systems*

Obviously much of what a person is working on as they grow and change is confidential. Confidentiality is an important safety mechanism that is built in to counseling, coaching, and other parts of the change process. So, we can't monitor everything that is *happening in the process.* But we do need to know whether the person is *engaging in the process.* Are they showing up and taking part? Are they trying? Are they invested? Are they building a track record of compliance in the program? The answers to these questions are essential in order to know if you are being betrayed or not.

Often, someone is needed to oversee the process to make sure compliance is steady. This can be whoever is appropriate, but someone should be in the driver's seat to be able to verify that the person is engaged in the process and say, "Yes. He is showing up and is engaged." That is often all we need to know. Sometimes more permission for divulging confidential information is allowed, and that can be great for others who are helping in some way. But, at the very least, we need some way to know the person is taking part in the processes we are depending on to help them change.

10. *If Applicable, Total Transparency*

This is the need for "no secrets." In many cases, deception has been the kernel that held a betrayal together. Duplicity, secrecy, lying, deception, hiding, covering up, and other behaviors have made it all work. For a future relationship to succeed, the person trying to change usually has to give up all secrecy and get totally transparent. This might include financial transparency, location transparency (even allowing their phone to be tracked), transparency permissions in communications (voice mails, emails, texts, social media), and transparency about meetings— especially in marriage betrayals. Full transparency is the only way to know what's really happening with someone and is often crucial for the other party to even begin to think about trusting again. If someone is not willing to have total transparency, you have to ask, "Why?"

There are some situations in which transparency cannot be total, but there better be a very good reason for it. Usually it is for the good of another party, not the betrayer. For example, their profession may involve confidentiality, but even then, you should be able to find out where the person was and what they were doing, if the other party remains protected. I will never forget the session where, after a sustained time of total transparency, I heard Drew say to Bella, "I don't quite know my schedule yet, but if you need to find me, just check the location tracker." And she said, "Oh . . . I don't ever use that anymore. I trust you now." It was an incredible moment of his having proven himself through transparency over time.

11. *Willingness to Be Questioned*

Naturally, a loss of trust sets people up to be suspicious. And often the suspicion is inaccurate, but understandable. The person who has been burned sees betrayal under every bush. This will take time to get over, and they need to be able to ask questions to get over it. Sometimes there are things that do not look good on the surface and have to be questioned.

For example, "You said you'd be here by 8:00 and you weren't. What were you doing?" and "What did you do last night," are normal questions.

When a person responds to normal questions with *defensiveness, it can be a bad sign, as the person is not fully submitting to the process.* Defensiveness should be dealt with and not enabled. If someone is going to rebuild trust, they must be open and not offended when another person asks about something that doesn't look exactly right to them. The betrayer must become a partner in the curiosity, not one who fights against another's wondering what was going on. People who are trying to become trustworthy must *welcome* being questioned, viewing it as a building block of trust and an opportunity to show they have nothing to hide. When they instead come back with the angry teenage response, "You just don't trust me!" the answer is, "You're right. I'm sorry. I don't fully trust you yet. But *I am trying to learn to trust you, and I need you to help me by being willing to answer anything I ask you and help me put to rest my questions or fears.*"

I have heard this angry or annoyed line a thousand times in business consulting situations and my hair always wants to catch fire: "So . . . are you questioning my integrity?"

I typically respond, "Well, I do have some questions, if that's what you mean. Are you above being questioned?" Then I continue, "I don't think any of us is above being questioned when something doesn't seem right. All of us should be open to being questioned and to be willing and helpful as we provide answers. So, may we continue?"

We all want to be trusted. But in betrayal situations, situations that don't look good should be able to be questioned. In positive scenarios, those questions are welcomed and seen as a great asset the betrayer has. In fact, I usually tell people trying to change that being open to audit at any time and answering questions will take them a long way toward regaining trust and showing others they have nothing to fear.

Signposts

These eleven points are monitoring signs in the process of watching someone become trustworthy. They are signs that their engagement in the change process is real, that they are really trying, and that there is real reason for hope. They are going for it!

Again, we are not looking for perfection. But if you look at the person who is trying to change and see most all of these elements in some fashion, and if the person is getting good marks, that's good news. That *is* what we see in people who really change. If you do not see the eleven indicators of engagement, you have a valid reason for questioning. And questioning is a good word, as sometimes there are reasons, but the questions should provide solutions to those as well. Watch the game from the bleachers and let these behaviors and indicators tell you if the process is most likely believable or not. These indicators are all easily identifiable and objective, so let the person who is trying to change show you they are pursuing change instead of making you guess.

Certainly, the ultimate proof is in the pudding. The real question is, "Is this person getting better at the *five elements of trust*?" But we're also looking for engagement in the growth process and structures that help them get better at the five elements. You can use the indicators in this chapter, from the bleachers, to tell you whether or not the person is truly working on themselves. These are great evaluators, in my experience. When they are present, I have hope. But when they're not, something should be addressed because chances are something is not going right. And, another great benefit is this: if they *are* fully engaged and change is not happening, you have to evaluate the process that is being used. They are working at it, but something else may be needed. If they are not working the process, then you can address that. But if they are and it is not working, different kinds of help, or more help, may be needed. It's one thing if a person is not taking the antibiotic and not improving. It is another thing altogether if they are dutifully taking it and not getting better. It may be time to change the medicine or the dosage.

Crawl, Walk, Run—and Give It Time

If I were going to add a seventh step to the process of repairing trust, it would be: "Crawl, walk, run." If everything we've looked at in the previous chapters is going well in a relationship, it's time to move forward slowly and incrementally.

If you are at a place where all is good, it's tempting to return the relationship to where it was before. Believe me, when things are getting better, it is so amazing, sometimes way better than it's ever been.

When you begin to trust again, begin in little steps.

When someone is doing well, you may be tempted to jump all in and think all the work is done. It may be, but you still don't know. So, when you begin to trust again, begin in little steps. Small steps. When someone meets the five essentials of trust in each step, especially as a track record is forming, then you can move to the next step in trusting them more. Personally, this may mean increasing contact and access to each other or ending a separation or whatever. In business, it may mean incremental increases until a person reaches a former level of responsibility, control, or trust. Regardless of the setting, do not go from nothing to everything, from zero to sixty, overnight. Get there gradually as trust is proven. Trust, and verify. Do not be discouraging to the person who is trying to change, but agree that restored trust will be a path. Let them know that your desire is to give it as soon as it feels right to give it, and their job is to accept that it will be given in steps.

If all of this happens, my prayer is that you have addressed a loss of trust well, worked through the issues, validated the progress and repair, and are enjoying the fruits of living in a better place than you ever have been.

SECTION 5

MOVING FORWARD

TWENTY

HOW NOT TO MAKE THE SAME MISTAKES AGAIN, PART 1

Now that you know what to look for as you determine whether the person in your life whom you need to change really is changing, let's turn our focus toward you. The person who broke your trust certainly bears responsibility for what he or she did, but have you considered that perhaps you made some mistakes too, as I mentioned at the end of chapter 16? Maybe you have some vulnerabilities that made you susceptible to trusting someone when you shouldn't have. I am in no way blaming you for what happened; I'm actually trying to help you keep it from happening again. That's why it's important to explore some of the reasons for misplaced trust, which is what this chapter and the next one are about.

Think for a moment about the immune system in the human body because we can learn some lessons about trust when we consider how it works. It's highly developed and complicated, but in the most basic terms, it protects us and keeps us healthy. When it works properly, it either keeps us from contracting a disease or infection or it fights off germs that have gained access to our bodies. One part of our immunity is innate; it's the equipment that comes from being human—skin, enzymes in tears and secretions, stomach acid, and other mechanisms to fight infection. It treats all germs and foreign

substances the same way and acts quickly when they try to enter the
body. The other part of our immune system is adaptive or special-
ized. This is the part that learns to recognize and respond to specific
germs and has the ability to remember them and fight them the next
time they try to enter the body.

We can learn a lot about trust from the immune system, specifically about misplaced trust, which is the focus of the next two chapters.
If you have misplaced trust in the past and suffered the consequences
of it, as probably everyone has, you don't want to do it again. This
chapter and the following one are designed to help you not to repeat
trust mistakes you have made in the past and to avoid ones you could
make in the future by building your "trust immunities."

**Misplaced trust happens in the heart, mind, and soul
like infection happens in the body.**

Misplaced trust happens in the heart, mind, and soul like infection happens in the body. We either don't have adequate "systems" in
our hearts, minds, and souls to protect us from untrustworthy people
to begin with or our immunities are down in some way, or we didn't
learn from past "trust infections" to develop the ability to recognize
and fight them off when they return.

I think it's safe to say that we would all like to be immune from
non-trustworthy people or to be able to recognize and resist them as
accurately as the immune system recognizes and fights a germ or a
virus. We'd like to deal with them as quickly and decisively as our
bodies fend off germs that enter them through a paper cut on a little
finger.

But we don't. Each of us can probably remember a time when we put our trust in the wrong person, group, or institution. The memories may still be painful. Who among us has never experienced betrayal in some way, and then asked ourselves, "How did that happen? What did I miss? Why did I trust that person to begin with?" Playing armchair quarterback and looking back at the "should haves" and self-judgment can be baffling and defeating. Other times, there was just *no way* to know, as some betrayers and con artists are *that* good. Think Bernie Madoff. Few people would have been able to see a problem coming with them. Either way, we can learn some lessons about ourselves that will make us more immune to mistrust in the future, at least to the extent that we can be. While I could write an entire book about reasons we misplace trust, for space purposes, I will simply lead you through five of the most common reasons people fall prey to the "toxins" of untrustworthy people with the immune system as our model. We'll look at the first two reasons in this chapter and at the others in the following chapter.

We can learn some lessons about ourselves
that will make us more immune to
mistrust in the future.

---

1. The Equipment Was Never Installed

Much of the strength of the immune system comes from day one. The fetus is being equipped from the very beginning of its development with what it will need to fight off infection. It gets some of this infection-fighting ability from its mother. Then later, as the child develops, parents and others build into it more immunities through nurturing attachments that build the immune system—proper nutrition, love and support, exercise, sleep habits, vaccinations, sunlight, and other things. In addition, the baby picks up the memory of what the mother has experienced and *learned* in her own immunities. This experience is loaded into the baby.

Similarly, parents teach their children early what kinds of people are safe and unsafe, what types to trust and not trust. The wisdom component parents (and others who guide them) teach children regarding character, spiritual values, life values and competencies, or which friends to hang around with functions like the immune system. It recognizes what is not okay to be in their life or in their soul. Then, wisdom knows to deal with any problems.

Parenting builds into a child the skills needed to deal with liars, bullies, people who use them or put them down, or those who otherwise betray them. It also teaches them how to build friendships with good people. These positive influences and skills help a child build defenses against "toxic" people or to deal with them once they show up. For example:

- "Don't talk to strangers."
- "Don't take candy from someone you don't know."
- "Don't go out on a date or even talk to someone online if that person has not come into your life through your known friends or safe circles."
- "Stay away from kids who use drugs."
- "Don't believe someone if they have lied to you in the past."
- "If someone is a bully, stay away from them."

Instructions such as these load the emotional and relational immune system. Teaching children boundaries, how to say no to protect themselves, how to have difficult conversations and address conflict, how to choose and develop healthy friendships—these build

into children a strong immune system for the future. It's like install-
ing a steering wheel into a car before it leaves the factory.

But often, *this factory loading does not happen in someone's development.* For many reasons, some people were not provided the parenting and family/community support they needed to help them avoid
dangerous people. Subsequently, people who are untrustworthy hurt
them.

What's worse, some children are not only deprived of the instruc-
tion they need to be able to recognize untrustworthy people, they are
actually treated in abusive ways, which make it seem "normal" to be
betrayed and hurt. They are used by a narcissistic and self-centered
parent who violates all of the five essentials of trust. This sets them
up to be used in future relationships. This happens partly because the
dynamics of the unhealthy relationship seem familiar. It also happens
because of their desperate need for love. Anyone who comes along can
cause them to have hope for love and they quickly give themselves
to that person. The absence of the intangible nutrients they need has
made their hearts vulnerable to anyone who pays them attention or
promises them something "good." Just like children, people who never
got the relational equipment they need are often quick to "attach" and
trust. They just trust the wrong people.

Not only do people from abusive or neglectful environments
often let bad people into their lives, they also are unable to recognize
the problem once the betrayer gets in. Remember how the immune
system works: once a toxin gets in, it recognizes it as such and deals
with it to protect itself. But think of people who are abused in some
way, recognize it as hurtful and cry, and then a parent says, "Shut up
or I'll give you something to cry about." Or what about a child who
grows up with an overdemanding parent with unreasonable expectations, always making them feel like they are not good enough? This
sets them up perfectly to later struggle under a demanding and toxic
boss, giving their all at work while constantly feeling betrayed and

never appreciated. The parent's harsh words talked them out of their immune response, which would have naturally said, "This is not good for me. I need to move on." Instead, they blame themselves and continue to grind it out. Abused people often blame themselves for the badness of the one who is actually the "bad guy." Their immune system is not recognizing the toxin, and it is not themselves.

**People from abusive backgrounds often tend to be set up
to trust abusive people in familiar patterns.**

In short, sadly, people from abusive backgrounds often tend to be set up to trust abusive people in familiar patterns. Things went badly for them in childhood, the "factory" where people are built, and the bad continues until they are healed and repaired.

The same principle applies to personal relationships in which someone has been gaslighted (talked out of their own reality) so much that they no longer trust their own feelings when they are with abusive, controlling, or manipulative people who do not take responsibility for how they hurt them. The recognition part of the immune response is not working. They just can't see that they are being victimized, and they often blame themselves.

Whatever the reasons people do not get the skills they need to be able to recognize toxins, it happens. It even happens with competent people we wouldn't think of as naïve. But in the right situation or context, they can be fooled just like anyone else. This often takes place in business settings, as smooth dealmakers seduce boards, partners, or investors who cannot recognize that something is wrong. The pattern recognition of their immune system is broken.

I once helped a board select a new company president and it came down to the final board interview with the final candidate that the selection committee had chosen. He had presented to the top executives and to the board previously and had wowed everyone with his intellect and charm. And, boy, was he good. Everything looked so polished, brilliant, and impressive. And it truly was. They were ready to hire him, pending this last group interview, which they asked me to attend.

The board members went around the table asking various questions. The candidate gave answers that were so insightful about their business, the future, his vision, and his plan. It really was impressive. He recounted his past successes and told about how he had done this or that in similar situations and knew how to deal with this one. He was really good.

But, in my mind, he was *too good*. He was just too perfect—too confident in a grandiose and narcissistic way, if you knew what to look for. I am not smarter than the executives in the room, but I do have a *lot* of professional experience with personality disorders and narcissistic high performers. I had no doubt I was looking at one. My "immune system recognition cells" were saying, "Toxic, toxic, toxic." I was about to throw up the more I listened to this self-aggrandizing model of all things wonderful and felt sick over the way the otherwise very smart people were falling in love with him. They had said as much to me before the meeting. "You will not believe this guy! He is so brilliant! He's the perfect leader for us." At first, I could not wait to meet him. But once I experienced him, I couldn't wait to help the board members see that he was totally untrustworthy.

When the time came for me to ask my questions, I had only one: "So, I can see how many of your strengths and experiences could benefit the business, no doubt. My question is about your weaknesses. How do you see them interacting with this position, and how would you plan to deal with the things you might struggle with or lack? What gaps would we need to help you with or prepare for?" I asked.

I will never forget his reaction: none. Crickets. He just stared at me, silently—for what seemed like a long time, looking a bit clueless, as though he didn't know what I was talking about.

I simply stared back.

Then, finally, he said, "Well, I guess my biggest weakness is that I am such a driver and love to get things done. I can leave some people behind, so I would have to make sure I am not leaving anyone too far behind me."

"I'm sorry," I said, "but moving forward to get things done sounds like a strength to me. I'm asking for a weakness, a gap." And I just looked at him and waited.

Then he said something to the effect of, "Well, it is a strength, but people who are not as fast can feel left behind."

"So, same question. Give me a weakness," I reiterated.

It never came. He simply laughed off the question in a charming way that amused the smitten ones in the group. Then, he was dismissed and we discussed him.

To a person, the board was ready to hire this man. He was so smart and talented and charming that they loved him.

"Please put me on record, in the minutes, as saying you should not hire him," I said. "I want to make sure you document this."

"What are you talking about," someone asked. "He is so talented and good. He will be awesome. How could you say 'no' to him?"

"Because, in his mind, he has never lost or had a failure. And I assure you, if you are not his first failure, you will be his next one," I answered.

We went on to discuss the situation further, but they did not buy what I was telling them and hired him anyway. Within a little over a year, he had driven the company into enormous messes and losses, and it took them another half a year to get rid of him. Culture problems, team problems, financial problems, and disappointed stakeholders were left in his wake. But the board had trusted him. Why?

For whatever reason, the board had no pattern recognition for this kind of personality type. To put this situation in the context of how deprivation sets people up for bad trust decisions, the company was in a needy place. They needed to be rescued from the loss of their previous leadership and were facing some challenging business situations. Like a hurting child, they were vulnerable to idealizing the first hero who showed up to rescue them, and they did. Their recognition immunities were not active because they were in a needy state, so their vulnerability made them, well, vulnerable.

Again, I'm not saying that I am smarter than the board members, as there were some very accomplished people on this board. But I did not "need" the candidate like they needed him, so I was not set up to *want to see what they wanted to see.* Plus, I've had a lot of clinical experience with narcissists. I've learned that they can't be trusted, as they will fail in several of the five essentials of trust.

So we can see how, during childhood and even later in life, abuse and being deprived of the equipment they need for healthy relationships can make people vulnerable to those who are not trustworthy.

2. We Don't Learn from Experience

You'll recall that, in the human body, the immune system is equipped at the factory, so to speak, to be able to fight off toxins and that it has not only innate immunities, but also adaptive ones. In other words, it *learns from experience.* Once it has interacted with a particular virus, bacteria, or disease, the system knows what that foreign agent looks like, marks it, and recognizes it in the future, because it has already developed the immune response and antibodies to kill it. Metaphorically, that's what was operating in the meeting with the board when they hired the wrong guy. I'd been in far too many situations with that kind of toxic leader or person to not recognize the pattern. I'd learned too many lessons from too many years of clinical practice and leadership consulting. (And a few personal betrayals, if I'm honest.)

In the same way the adaptive immune system learns from each exposure to infection and toxins, we are to be learning from our relationship experience. We need to be learning along the way to see patterns and avoid them. We should feel something similar to what the philosopher Nietzsche said, "I am not upset that you lied to me, I am upset that from now on I can't believe you."

I remember a treatment group I had years ago where a woman said, "I get it. I have been married to nine abusive men, and I am not going to ever do it again!"

Someone else in the group replied, "Oh, stop it, Mary. You have not been married to nine abusive men. You have been married to the same abusive man with nine different names." Wow, such wisdom about recognizing patterns.

Each experience we have with a person should teach us what their patterns are, but they should also show us what *our* patterns are. We should ask ourselves, "What pattern do *I* have that makes me vulnerable to not seeing what others see in this person? Where is my recognition broken in a way that causes me to trust people who are untrustworthy? Why can I be hurt more than a few times by the same person, or why can I keep trusting the same kind of person over and over?" These are great and important questions, and the answers can be myriad:

■ You were set up for vulnerability by family of origin patterns you were unable to see as a child, and they became normal for you. You had an emotionally or otherwise untrustworthy parent or parents or other significant relationships in which you learned that dysfunction or abuse was "normal" or that you were to blame for it.

- Sometimes this happens not in families of origin, but in adult relationships that have broken your recognition abilities. This is similar to the Stockholm syndrome, when an abusive relationship involves an imbalance of power and a bond is created between the abuser and the abused in the midst of it as the victim begins to trust the abuser or the person holding them psychologically captive.

- You have a history of being talked out of your perceptions, feelings, thoughts, or realities. This is called "gaslighting," and people who have been gaslighted are often unable to give value to their own realities. So, when the next person comes along and talks them out of how they feel or what they see in the relationship, they doubt themselves and stay in it. One of my favorite Bible verses is Hebrews 5:14: "But solid food is for the mature, who because of practice have their senses trained to distinguish between good and evil" (NASB). This is immune system recognition. But if you have been "gaslighted out of your senses," this ability doesn't work well.

- You have never allowed yourself to see the "bad" in a parent or someone with whom you had a significant formative relationship. For example, some people see one or both parents or other developmental relationships as "all good." They cannot see faults in these people, so they cannot see faults when they later encounter similar personalities. If they idealized their mother, or father, for example, and saw them as "all good," never recognizing their weaknesses or admitting how the parent may have hurt or disappointed them, they see some later men or women the same way. This makes them blind to those people's deficiencies. Being able to see people in our past clearly with resolution and forgiveness is key to being able to learn what hurts and what doesn't.

■ Sometimes, we have not seen ourselves accurately, so we haven't learned to see others clearly. If we have certain faults and, as Jesus teaches, haven't gotten the "log out of our own eye," then we can't see other people's issues clearly. If someone is passive, for example, and hasn't faced their own passivity, they may not be able to see how aggressive and abusive someone else is. They might actually be attracted to that person because they possess the "assertiveness" that they lack.

Similarly, if someone has self-image issues or narcissistic leanings, wanting to see themselves as "ideal," they can be attracted to narcissistic people who are *way* worse than they are and get betrayed greatly. Or, if someone is lonely and needy, they tend to idealize others, thinking they are just what they need, seeing that person as "ideal." That's what happened with the board that needed a president for their company. The more unmet needs we have, the more vulnerable we are to trusting non-trustworthy people. As Proverbs 27:7 says, "A person who is full refuses honey, but even bitter food tastes sweet to the hungry" (NLT). When we have high needs, we can make bitter, untrustworthy people look pretty good. Our need causes us to see what we want to see in them. If we are somewhat controlling, domineering, or place high demands on others, passive people might not say "no" to us or be honest with us. Then, when they have finally had enough, they will betray us and turn against us in anger.

There are many reasons our immune system does not learn from experience. Those reasons are too many to list here, but suffice it to say that whatever is hurt or undeveloped in us makes us vulnerable to not being able to see as well as we need to. This is why it behooves us to look at our own issues and experiences with people—so our "eye can see clearly" as we evaluate others. The healthier we become, the better we get at seeing what might be right in front of us.

As I stated earlier, this is in no way meant to blame the victim. *The betrayer of trust is the one responsible for betrayal, period.* I am simply saying here that we can grow in our abilities to spot betrayers when they come along and be less likely to be fooled by them. This isn't true in all cases, but it is still possible for us to develop sharper vision.

TWENTY-ONE

HOW NOT TO MAKE THE SAME MISTAKES AGAIN, PART 2

I hope the previous chapter was helpful to you in terms of making better trust decisions in the future. In this chapter, let's continue to explore more reasons people misplace their trust. The better you understand these, the better you can protect yourself from them or work to overcome them.

3. Lack of Boundaries and Boundary-Setting Skills

One of the most important aspects of the immune system is its ability to fight off the toxins and make sure they do not further infect us. From less invasive measures to more significant ones, the immune system has a cascading bag of tools to protect the body.

It first uses something low-level, like saliva or stomach acid, to destroy a toxin. Tears, mucus, and even skin perform low-level immune functions, catching antigens before they enter the body. When they do their job, people never even consciously know anything has happened.

In many ways, the immune system is to our bodies what boundaries are to our hearts and minds. We need low-level skills in personal relationships, ways to protect ourselves against infractions. One of these skills would be the ability to easily see an issue and talk about it with someone else: "That didn't feel good. I want to talk about it with you." Or, "This doesn't seem right. Can you explain to me why you put the money in that account instead of the regular one?" You get my point. The use of basic, direct, assertive (not aggressive) conversation to address a problem is a low-level immune response. It is very normal. As we have seen earlier, if the other person owns what they have done, problem gone. Immune functioning is working. Trust saved.

The immune system is to our bodies what boundaries are to our hearts and minds.

Being able to talk about something that bothers us, quickly, keeps problems from growing larger and prevents us from trusting people who are not trustworthy. Many trust betrayals should have been nipped in the bud, but little things were ignored or enabled because someone was conflict avoidant. They didn't have the boundaries that enabled them to say, "This can't continue." We all need to develop the skills to deal with conflict before it leads to a meltdown.

I remember hiring someone a long time ago. She was moving to a new apartment, and the person approving her application called me to validate some financial information. The salary number she had given was a lie, and I told her I would not confirm it. She was a little miffed and did not quite understand why I would be so "rigid" about a "small thing." But, the young and less experienced me made a mistake. While I did bring up the issue, I did not immediately see the bigger trust warning sign. I should have fired her on the spot, but I didn't. Later, I found out why I should have let her go. My immune system learned a lesson. I could have avoided a bigger problem that came later. This is an example of a low-level, saliva-like intervention—a simple conversation and *then acting on it*, would have saved me from later problems with her.

In the body, when low-level interventions aren't enough, the immune system quickly sends other cells to help fend off infection. Likewise, when a simple conversation and boundaries don't solve a problem, higher-level boundaries and protective strategies are needed. It's *time to enlist others and respond with stronger action to stop the infection*. Get wise, skilled, trustworthy people around you, name the problem, and let them help you with it if you can't do it alone. This is a next level "intervention." When we are at the point of needing to bring in others, the conversations are more difficult, as you are dealing with stronger "toxins." But the advanced immune response of facing the problem in this next level of confrontation with others will help contain the problem. These are stronger boundaries.

Being able to talk about something that bothers us, quickly, keeps problems from growing larger and prevents us from trusting people who are not trustworthy.

So remember, at this level, the immune system makes sure it clearly *names the toxin, in the clear daylight view of the ones who will help*. This is the skill I was talking about earlier in the book, when I wrote about the need to honestly "blame" the person accurately, to name the infraction and not let them off the hook. And remember, in both reconciliation and repair, it's necessary to clearly articulate how the five essentials of trust have been violated and to have people who will help you to help the betrayer see it and also help you to contain it from getting worse or continuing. When the one who betrayed you owns what they've done, then you can move toward resolution. When they don't, you invoke whatever consequences are necessary.

Identifying a problem and protecting yourself from it at this level requires the abilities to name it and blame it, and to use others to help. But sometimes, if someone has grown up without learning how to confront issues in people, or if they were hurt when they did, this basic ability to lean into difficult issues like this is missing. They do not have the boundaries, confrontational skills, or abilities they need, or the community around them to help, or the boundaries to reinforce the immune response. So, misplaced trust is able to happen and even grow. This is why boundaries and boundary-setting skills are so important, as is the ability to engage others when your individual attempts are not strong enough.

Many years ago, I was flying through a city where a friend and his wife lived. I wanted to see them, so I called and they invited me to their family dinner. This was a great family with really healthy family dynamics. They had four kids, all of whom were a joy to be around.

During dinner they asked me how a mutual friend of ours was doing. The truth was that he had had an affair and had wrecked his life. I felt a little squeamish discussing the reality of the situation in front of the children, ages 5 to 13. So, I tried to describe the situation in roundabout terms—not being direct and using big words—in an effort to talk to the adults in a way that the children wouldn't grasp what I was saying. I'll never forget what the nine-year-old daughter said. She interrupted me and, with a confused look on her face, asked, "What language are you speaking?"

I almost fell over. Her question was *so* insightful and accurate. I remember thinking, *This kid is never going to fall for anyone's BS. She has a monitor inside of her that is able to see it, to name it, and to confront it. I doubt she'll ever have a lot of misplaced trust issues.*

To our point, she had grown up with parents who treated each other with respect and were open and honest with each other. And they were building those abilities into their children. Just as bank tellers are trained to instantly spot counterfeit currency by handling real money, the daughter had been raised around real relationships and was able to address and confront something that was not normal.

But many people have not had the opportunity to observe and develop the ability to see a problem, name it, confront it, and protect themselves from it. It takes skills to do those things, and people have to have an environment in which to learn how to have good boundaries and confrontation and containment skills. Those who do not will encounter betrayers who can easily take advantage of them.

For more information on boundaries and instructions on how to set them, I've written an entire book with Dr. John Townsend, called *Boundaries*, which explores this subject in depth. For now, though, let me simply say that being able to quickly address issues that arise and having the boundaries to say, "I do not allow myself to be treated that way, so until we can address it and clear it up, I can't move forward," is vital in the arena of trust. Without setting and enforcing boundaries, and sometimes use others to help, the virus of misplaced trust can infect a relationship. Proper boundaries, however, are like a strong immune system—they'll keep mistrust from going too far.

4. Lack of Early Antibodies

Have you ever known anyone who simply cannot believe someone broke their trust? They are stunned that such a thing could happen. And when that person breaks their trust again, they are just as surprised as they were the first time. We see this dynamic frequently when people, who are often loving and responsible, get sucked in by an untrustworthy person. They are surprised over and over again when the same person isn't trustworthy because their basic worldview does not include people who deceive and hurt others. So when one of those people comes along, they can't recognize and understand what is happening. They then think they can love the person out of it. But they simply are not equipped to deal with it. They are naïve, in the most innocent meaning of the word, a person "showing a lack of experience, wisdom, or judgment," according to the *Oxford English Dictionary*. In other words, they have never experienced being lied to, deceived, or cheated. They don't know that people who treat others badly exist.

Think back to the immune system and remember that an incredible part of its strength comes from learning how to deal with various viruses, bacteria, bugs, and foreign substances *from having dealt with them before. Catching something gives the immune system the ability to fight it off the next time around. It learns and says, "Ha! I see you and you are not going to get me this time!"* This is why research shows that parents who don't allow their children to have normal interactions with nature, dirt, and the world keep their children's immune systems from learning early how to deal with all sorts of antigens. Those kids tend to get sick a lot later. They are "naïve" in immunity, having never encountered many germs and therefore not knowing how to deal with them.

When I was a child, my mother would make me spend the night with friends who caught a childhood disease so I would get it too. She would say, "It's a lot better to have it as a child than as an adult, so go catch it and get it over with." In many ways, she was right. (Not a good idea for all disease, but you get the point.) I also remember when I first started flying a lot, 150,000 miles a year, for my work. I used to get so many colds and crappy little bugs. This happened every year, until it didn't. After a number of years, it simply stopped. I have to assume I had caught everything I could catch! My system was no longer naïve. Now, I rarely get anything, thank God, and I cannot attribute it to any great health program that I am on other than normal self-care. The reason has to be that I have, like a pediatrician, been exposed to most of what is out there.

Some of the people who get hit the hardest by betrayal are the nicest, most loving, most responsible people you could meet. Why? Because they think everyone is like they are. They think everyone is good and can be trusted. When those people cannot be trusted, the wonderful people keep getting surprised, so they get hit with betrayal again. Even after confronting the problem and getting an apology or having a "convincing" conversation, they are surprised yet again the next time it happens. They just can't believe it. They really can't.

Perhaps you're one of these people. Your personal immune system may never have been exposed to deception, irresponsibility, selfishness, incompetency, or other traits before now. And this leaves you vulnerable. The solution to this problem is multifold, including experience, but you really, really need a "wingman" or two, another set of eyes when you make important trust decisions. And, it's time to accept reality: not everyone is as honest and trustworthy as you are.

Learning not to repeat mistakes of misplaced trust is about learning from experience. This is called wisdom.

Learning not to repeat mistakes of misplaced trust is about *learning from experience. This is called wisdom.* We gain wisdom from experience, but your own experiences are not the only source of wisdom. You can also get it from other people's experiences and through studying wisdom literature, like the Proverbs, or reading other material about character functioning and whom to trust and whom to avoid (like this book ☺). You can also gain wisdom from learning settings, such as groups with other people who are going through similar situations. Think Al-Anon, DivorceCare, leadership groups with other executives who deal with people issues, or good HR training. As I mentioned at the beginning of the book, trust is the fuel for all of life, so it's vital for us to learn about people and to understand patterns that make them untrustworthy.

One of the most important life skills we can ever develop is the ability to judge character.

One of my favorite manuals for avoiding misplaced trust is Psalm 101. There, David basically says, "There are people I will not trust, and I'm going to stay far away from. There are also those I will get close to because they are good people." Here are the traits and kinds of people he teaches us to avoid:

- "Faithless people" who do not persevere in their commitments (v. 3).
- Perversity, which means "twisted," like people who "twist" love into sick love or manipulation or other lack of purity in action. They "distort" things into being something they shouldn't be (v. 4).
- Any kind of evil (v. 4).
- People who slander "their neighbor in secret," meaning to gossip or talk behind another's back (v. 5).
- Haughty eyes that look down on others with a proud heart, which is basically narcissism (v. 5) or judgmentalism.
- Deceit or lying of any kind (v. 7).

David goes on to say he will hang out with and be ministered to by faithful people and those "whose walk is blameless," meaning that they walk in the way of integrity (v. 6). He will choose well because he knows what to look for.

If your background is naïve, learn what bad people look like and what they do. Do not be surprised by them when they show up in your life, and develop a strong immunity to them.

5. Lack of a Tribe, Markers, Supporters, and Fighters

One fact we know about the immune system is that it does not send a cell out on its own. Cells work together. The same is true when people are vulnerable to giving misplaced trust. We need others at every step of the way.

We need the ability to see a toxin, name it, and mark it, just as the immune system does. We have all had the experience of having a single friend who has been looking for a relationship for a long time and then says, "I have met the one! He [or she] is awesome! You have to meet them. Can you go to dinner on Friday?"

You agree and have dinner. Afterward, when the awesome date is gone and you and your spouse or other friends are alone with your excited friend, you have to turn to him or her and say, "What are you *thinking?*"

What you mean is that they have picked a nutcase, but they can't see it. They are too smitten, but the person will be a real problem if the relationship continues. Not to sound judgmental, but there are just some people that it does not take a Ph.D. to diagnose. They simply are not a good choice for a significant relationship. But the one who thinks they're awesome, in their state of need or denial or idealization of someone's one or two strong qualities, doesn't see the other issues. And *they need your eyes.* Just as the immune system puts a lot of eyes on a toxin to see it and name it to protect you against it, you need friends and other sets of eyes to help you protect yourself emotionally and relationally. Otherwise, you may step into an area of vulnerability. As the Bible says, "For by wise counsel you will

wage your own war, and in a multitude of counselors *there is* safety"
(Prov. 24:6 NKJV).

In addition, certain confrontations, difficult conversations, and
other interventions are very hard to do, and they sometimes involve a
lot of fear and pain. To do them, people need support from others, just
as the immune system needs support from other cells. And there are
times in people's lives where they simply do not have the support they
need and they can't put up the immune response that they need either.

There are also times when betrayal means a fight has to be put
up to protect you. Earlier, we looked at stories involving corporate
boards and stories about who needed professional help or protection.
Sometimes, when people do not feel they have access to people who
will stand with them and help protect them, they are susceptible to
betrayal. To stand up and protect oneself from and in the midst of
betrayal may mean you need a lot of help. Some people don't have that
kind of community and support and it leads them to being vulnerable, stuck in misplaced trust. Or they might have it available, but are
too afraid or ashamed to let anyone know they need it. Either way,
they are immunocompromised. They need help. Don't ever be afraid
or ashamed to ask for the help you need.

Equip Yourself

Dealing with problematic people and betrayal is a two-edged sword.
While the people who betray us certainly have issues, we do too.
Usually, we didn't cause their issues and are in no way responsible for
what they did, but I will say again that we may have some patterns
that make us vulnerable to those types of people, and we would do
well to address them. For example, as long as there are controlling
people in the world, others do well to develop strong boundaries. If
they don't, the controllers will continue to control them. But when
people grow in their ability to say "no," the control ends.

When people have been betrayed and hurt and you try to help them work on themselves and get stronger, some may say you are "victim blaming." *Nothing could be further from the truth. I blame only the betrayer for the betrayal, and if you have been betrayed, then you should too. Do NOT accept responsibility for the way someone else has hurt you. That is on them.* But it is not "victim blaming" but "victim empowering" to grow wiser in finding out how to spot untrustworthy people and the patterns that make all of us a little less than immune to them. A strong immune system is vital for life. It keeps the bad agents from getting in or helps you fight them off quickly when they do. Develop your immunity in the people department and you will be much, much safer.

CONCLUSION

Hopefully, as you've made your way through this book, you've real-ized how vital good trust skills are and you are already growing in them. As I mentioned in the introduction, trust is the fuel for all of life. It makes everything in life work, especially relationships. A healthy ability to trust the right people and the skills to avoid trust-ing the wrong ones are integral to positive, healthy relationships, both personally and professionally. And healthy relationships are key to your thriving as an individual.

Though I'd like to believe the information in this book will give you complete immunity to bad trust decisions in the future, I can't make that promise. My hope, though, is that you are much better equipped to trust well now that you've read the book than you were before you came across it. You have within these pages a lot of proven advice you can turn to next time you wonder, "Can I trust this person—or not?" I don't think it would be a bad idea for this book to be required reading every time anyone enters a new relationship!

If you're like most people, your experiences with trust haven't been perfect. Maybe you've been extremely hurt or damaged due to a betrayal. Perhaps you've had more bad trust encounters than good ones. If so, I hope you'll read this book more than once. Make it a manual for your life for a while. Dig deep into its truths, apply its principles, and work through the models it presents. They're designed to help you succeed, as the saying goes, "from the bedroom to the boardroom." Whether you need to repair trust in your marriage, your extended family, a group of friends, your church, a small business, or a major corporation, what you've learned in this book will serve you well.

In every relationship you develop in the future, I hope you'll remember these words: *understanding, motive, ability, character,* and *track record*. As you now know, these are the essentials of trust. These are the qualities that, when lived out well, will provide the fuel your life and relationships need to go somewhere wonderful.

ADDITIONAL REASONS FOR
MISPLACED TRUST

If this were a book on infectious diseases and their immune response, we would not be able to address all the reasons people can be susceptible to illness because there are just too many. And in terms of the weaknesses that make us susceptible to relational trust betrayals, we have explored several of them already, but we have not exhausted them all. If you are interested in other issues that cause people to misplace trust, here's an annotated list.

- *Emotional Isolation:* Feeling alone and isolated can cause some people to trust the wrong individuals or groups for several reasons. Their need and desire for connection make them cut corners and ignore clear warning signs. The same principle can apply in business settings. Being "without a deal" can be so scary that people enter into bad agreements or hire the wrong person because their need is so great.

- *Feeling Powerless and Lack of Boundaries:* If someone does not feel empowered to say "no" to abuse, gaslighting, control, blame, and other harmful dynamics, they have poor boundaries and cannot keep untrustworthy people away. Those who cannot be trusted can work their way in to the person's life because of the inability to confront and set limits and/or the inability to say "no" to negative treatment. They may know that something feels "off" in the relationship, yet they do not address it because of fear or inability.

- *Needing the "Ideal":* People who don't feel okay about themselves sometimes need to be connected to someone who appears "awesome" or who makes them feel that they themselves are wonderful. These deficits in one's self-image propel them to seek relationships with those who make them feel important, special, or good, or to be connected to someone of status or power. The problem is that, often, the people they connect themselves to are manipulators and flatterers who make the person feel good so they can get something, or use the person to make themselves feel good. Either way, it doesn't work. Looking for the perfect person or gravitating toward people that make you feel you are more ideal is a setup for misplaced trust.

- *Taking the Rescue Bait:* This dynamic sets people up for faulty trust in relationships. They often feel mistreated by one person, and then someone else comes along and tells them how wonderful they are and how awful it is that the other person can't see their wonderful-ness. They believe the flattery and join the rescuer, the one who saved them from the bad marriage, the bad boss, the bad friend, or whomever. In reality, they are being manipulated. The rescuer will be on their side until some disappointment occurs in the relationship, and then the cycle will begin again as trust breaks down. Many second marriages and new jobs begin this way.

■ *Merger Fantasies:* Sometimes we feel something is missing in us, and we will be drawn to someone who possesses what we don't have. We may be a bit fearful of the world, but have a lot to offer, and someone else is full of confidence and can benefit from the good things we bring to their life. Because of our fear, we "merge" with the confident person so we can feel complete or whole. But because of the need that drives the merger, we can't see other aspects of the person—the untrustworthy ones. The need to merge and complete oneself blinds us to who the other person really is. There is nothing wrong with complementary relationships, as we all have different strengths. But to let the need for completion blind us to someone untrustworthy and lead us to trust them is a problem. It's common but destructive. Many times, women who have been victimized and find it hard to stand up for themselves and set boundaries succumb to or are even attracted to "strong," assertive men. They feel "protected" around someone who can stand up in life. But often, these men are narcissistic and controlling, and the women soon begin to feel the results of those issues.

■ *Someone from Your Past:* This is a huge reason for misplaced trust. It is one of the oldest psychological patterns known, and it basically says this: if someone in your formative past, such as a parent, had issues, and you have never dealt with them, you will be blind to them in the present. If you aren't blind to them, you'll overreact to them. In other words, people have unfinished business with Mom or Dad, and then someone like Mom or Dad comes along. In those relationships, patterns from the past repeat themselves because people are in denial about their past and how it affected them. I know people who come from horrible backgrounds and are fantastic at choosing people to trust because they have appropriately "blamed" their parents, at least in their heads. When they do, they get the badness where it belongs and can be seen: on the other person. If someone never sees that Mom was critical or Dad was sometimes mean and angry, the badness is never placed on the person it belongs to, and that sets people up for not being able to see it in others. But when they finally allow themselves to be honest about their past, they can not only forgive and love their parents, they can also see others clearly, as they are, instead of being in denial about people who have the same issue. How many times have you heard someone going through or after a divorce say something like, "I married someone like my father. I just never saw it"? There is a reason the Bible teaches us to confess our sins and the sins of our fathers (Leviticus 26:40) and warns us about the practice of repeating "the traditions of the elders" (Mark 7:1-13 csb). We must see things that are generational in nature and break their chains by admitting them, forgiving them, and moving on.

- *Insecure Attachment Styles:* I explained these in chapter 10, so I won't go into detail here. However, insecure attachment styles are a big reason many people put their trust in the wrong people. This happens personally as well as in business.

- *Rescue Fantasies:* Rescue fantasies are at work when you see someone's issues but feel bad for that person and believe your love can change them. Or you believe your leadership can develop them, that they just haven't ever had a boss or partner like you. I do not mean this in a demeaning way. In personal relationships, great leaders, people developers, and loving individuals heal and help others every day. We can and do heal each other, thank God. But as the saying goes, "It takes two to tango." Your wish to rescue someone may be greater than their wish to change, and if you are the only one trying, you'll end up disappointed. As I noted earlier, you have to see that the other person is engaged in the process, otherwise your attempts to help will probably be in vain.

- *Victim Thinking:* Some people are stuck in a powerless mindset, thinking there is little that they can do about a troubled relationship. Whereas this was probably true in a power imbalanced relationship in which they experienced being victimized, they still feel that way and have not yet begun to be empowered with a different mindset. When people have this mindset, untrustworthy individuals can have them by the horns, so to speak. But, as we have seen, there is a *lot* you can do when faced with untrustworthiness, once you find the right support and get the right kind of wisdom and help.

- *Guilt:* Sometimes, in relationships with certain untrustworthy people, the one who is being let down or betrayed feels like the situation is their fault in some way. "I should have done such-and-such." Or, "I did not help them like I should have," or, or, or . . . The problem is exacerbated by the fact that many deceivers and betrayers are really good at blame, so the guilt is easy to come by. If you are guilt-prone, make sure that tendency doesn't keep you from addressing problems.

- *Too High Pain Tolerance:* Sometimes, when people come from a background of difficult relationships or are overly responsible, they have learned to put up with way, way too much before pulling the trigger on taking action. Sometimes they won't even initiate a conversation when needed. They just suck up the pain, anger, or betrayal and either aren't aware of their feelings or are not listening to them. This person bugs them in some way, but they continue to stomach the pain or distress. Check your pain tolerance, and if you have distress in a relationship, do not ignore it any more than you would ignore a stomachache. Pay attention; pain is there for a reason.

ACKNOWLEDGMENTS

When I am asked, "How long did it take you to write this book?" I often say, "The work writes the book, and then at some point I have to type it."

I am not really what I think of as an "author." I am a practitioner who happens to take what the real work teaches me and then at some point writes it down. That is so true here with *Trust*. The topic of *Trust* is one that has been front and center in both my clinical and consulting practices for decades. As a clinician, I was trained that it was the key to all human development, as you will read more about here. But what I discovered in my consulting practice in business was that people and businesses would do well to have an actual "formula" or paradigm to think about how to make trust tangible. If they had a model of how trust works, they could activate it, discern it, build trust, and avoid mistakes in trusting the wrong people. So, years ago, I set out to build a usable "trust paradigm" for my clients, as is reflected here. Researching, developing, and using the specific model in this book has taken a decade or more. To be real and valuable, a model has to "work" in real settings and lives, and that takes time.

But apart from the process described above, at some point, a book actually has to get written down and published. And there are a few people I want to thank specifically for their role in helping get this one written and brought to completion:

To Jan Miller and Shannon Marven, my literary agents at Dupree Miller. You make it all work. Jan, for the incredible agency and team you have built and all you have done for my publishing efforts, thank you. From our first meeting with Tony, I knew that you were the one to help me. And Shannon, what can I say? You bring it all to fruition. I always tell people there is no one I have met in the publishing world who is more competent in making it all work than you. And with this book, there were a lot of hills to climb logistically, editorially, and otherwise, upon which you paved the way up and over each bump. I will always be grateful to you.

To Daisy Hutton, my publisher at Hachette. You saw the vision for this book and decided to join it, and stewarded it to publication. Thank you for your confidence and trust in this material and your help along the way. Your connection to the content and paradigm and enthusiasm for what it can do for people was fueling.

To my content team at DrCloud.com, Greg and Alby. The countless hours of video production that we have done on so many topics that touch upon *Trust* have sharpened the message and the content for this book. You guys always make me better.

To Tori, my wife, and Olivia and Lucy, our daughters. You more than anyone else know the time it took this year to get it done, and your carving out windows in our time together by flexing schedules, as well as your support, was monumental. This one was not easy to get done and you helped me more than I can say.

And almost without saying, I have to thank my clients who over the years have trusted me in their journeys. You inspire me, and also you have put real legs to this material as you have put it to use over the years, and helped me make it better all along the way. Thank you for opening up your lives, war rooms, and entire companies to work on *Trust*. You are awesome, and I am always inspired by your trustworthiness for the people you lead and how you through your businesses make life better for so many. And for those organizations who have asked me to speak on this topic, your feedback has been invaluable.

And finally, the trustworthy friends in my life. You have shown me your understanding, motive, ability, character, and track record over so many years. You more than anyone have taught me that when people exhibit these qualities, trust works. You have healed me and made me better. I will never not benefit from who you have been to me. Thank you.

Henry Cloud, Ph.D.
Los Angeles, 2022

ABOUT THE AUTHOR

DR. HENRY CLOUD is an acclaimed leadership expert, clinical psychologist, and *New York Times* best-selling author. His forty-five books, including the iconic *Boundaries*, have sold nearly twenty million copies worldwide. He has an extensive executive coaching background and experience as a leadership consultant, devoting the majority of his time to working with CEOs, leadership teams, and executives to improve performance, leadership skills, and culture.